Torah, Tarot & Tantra

TORAH, TAROT & TANTRA
A Guide to Jewish Spiritual Growth

William Blank

COVENTURE

Boston   London

Coventure Ltd Boston and London
25 New Chardon Street #8748
Boston, Massachusetts 02114

Publisher and General Editor, Sisa Sternback

Library of Congress Cataloging-in-Publication Data

Blank, William.

    Torah, tarot, and tantra: a guide to Jewish spiritual growth William Blank.
    p.   cm.
    Includes bibliographical references and index.
    ISBN 0-904575-52-7. — ISBN 0-904575-51-9 (pbk.)
    1. Jewish way of life.   2. Occultism—Religious aspects—   Judaism.
I. Title.
BM723.B49   1991   90-8773
296.7'4—dc20   CIP

Printed in the United States of America on recycled acid-free paper.
Set in Garamond.

..."Had Jerusalem been located at the foot of the Himalayas, monotheistic philosophy would have been modified by the tradition of oriental thinkers. Thus, our intellectual position situated as it is between Athens and Jerusalem is not an ultimate one. Providence may some day create a situation which would place us between the river Jordan and the river Ganges, and the problem of such an encounter will be different from that which Jewish thought underwent when meeting Greek philosophy..."

—Abraham Joshua Heschel
God in Search of Man, 1955

Contents

List of Experiences

Acknowledgements

All the people to whom I want to give special thanks are women. I will pass on interpreting this datum here. Sisa Sternback, publisher of Sigo/Coventure Presses saw the potential of the book when it was still in an embryonic state and midwifed it through its gestation. My editor, Lyndsay Smith, coached it through difficult labor, contractions and transitions. Barbara Shor provided much needed intervention and guidance when the manuscript was still in its first trimester. Most of all, my wife Wendy has been totally supportive of this project throughout its many stages. And my daughters, Jessie, Eva, and Lana gave me the sunshine that has kept it all going.

Introduction

There is a paradox about spiritual experience: it is totally transforming, but it is very subtle. The changes it facilitates are difficult to describe, yet intense spiritual experiences can rock you to your very core. Intense spiritual experiences hit you over the head like a mallet, but no one else can even perceive the bruise.

This is a spiritual guidebook, a tool to help you along a spiritual path. That path is a set of teachings and practices which foster spiritual experiences. A spiritual experience is transforming — it can change you.

There are many different spiritual paths on this planet. Each one inspires unique spiritual experiences. Though each is unique, all have much in common.

If you stay on a path long enough, that path will lead you to its ultimate experience and your radical transformation.

The ultimate experience has various names: the experience of God, the experience of the Oneness of God, the experience of the unity of all things, of infinite nothingness, of boundless compassion, of enlightenment, of bliss, or the experience of an ultimate "something else."

A spiritual guidebook is successful if it helps you move along your spiritual path toward the ultimate experience.

The "ultimate experience" is the ultimate meaning of life.

Deep spiritual experiences are rare. Many people have them but do not understand them. As a result, they either ignore the experience they have had, or else they do not appreciate its significance. Other people do not have them. As a result, they may not believe they exist. This book can help you encounter these experiences as well as to understand them.

Most useful spiritual guidebooks derive from the lineage of a particular spiritual path. The subtleties of spiritual transformative experience *usually* take generations or more to develop. The longer and more manifest the lineage, the more likely that the spiritual text can help you experience something ultimate.

This particular spiritual guidebook belongs to Jewish tradition.

This book's title, *Torah, Tarot and Tantra*, refers to three diverse spiritual paths. Torah is the central spiritual guidance of the Jewish tradition, revealed to Moses thousands of years ago. Tarot is a particular set of cards which developed in Medieval Europe, whose pictures are the signposts of a process of deep self-exploration. Tantra is an ancient set of Hindu and Buddhist teachings which maintains that the universe is permeated by a subtle energy that links each individual to God.

This spiritual guidebook is an explication of the Way of Torah. It is different from other explications of Torah in that it recognizes that other spiritual paths can frequently illuminate Torah in new, wonderful, and unexpected ways. The experiences Torah facilitates emerge easily by considering how the other peoples of the world deal with the same conundrum of human experience.

At 4000 years old, the Jewish tradition is arguably the spiritual tradition currently in active use with the longest record of uninterrupted maintenance. Although it has never attracted more than a tiny percentage of the world's people, it has had an immense influence on the spiritual life of half the world.

The Jewish spiritual tradition begins with the experience of Abraham, the founder and primordial ancestor of the Jewish people. Abraham experiences the Oneness of God and communicates that experience to his tribe-clan. The tradition that Abraham began has continued through an unbroken chain of Abraham's spiritual and physical descendants, throughout the unfolding of Western and Middle Eastern history.

The ultimate Jewish spiritual experience is the "experience of God" or "the experience of the Oneness of God."

Any attempt to describe the experience of the Oneness of God limits it to something less than what it really is. The experience is ineffable. Words struggle to grasp it, but ultimately fail. It can only be experienced.

The *experience of* God is different from the *belief in* God. Whether God exists or not, there is an *experience of* God which is so powerful that all other human experiences pale by comparison. Anyone who has the experience is transformed radically.

If you had never seen a roller coaster but you had heard tales about the existence of these "incredible riding-down-steep-hills-on-track-machines," you might either "believe" or "disbelieve" the stories about how wonderful they are. But if you wanted the "experience of" a roller coaster, then you'd resolve to find a map to the nearest amusement park and to begin the journey.

This Jewish spiritual guidebook is an invitation to both Jews and non-Jews to experience Jewish spirituality. To "get on and ride."

Jewish spirituality is tied tightly to the Jewish tribe. For the most part, only Jews have worked within the Jewish spiritual lineage, and Jewish spiritual texts have been directed to Jews alone. This book is unusual within the Jewish tradition in that it offers its fruits freely to anyone who feels a resonance with it.

This Jewish spiritual guidebook presents a new Jewish theology.

Over the last 4000 years, the Jewish spiritual lineage has interacted with the civilizations of the Ancient Near East, the Classical Greco-Roman world, the Christian European World, and the Moslem Middle East. As it studies each culture, it celebrates their commonalities and underscores their differences. This process is called "theology," or "the way we understand the experience of God."

Now for the first time, the Jewish spiritual lineage finds itself in close proximity to the religions of the Far East. Far Eastern religions offer spiritual paths oriented to direct personal experience, whose very "exoticness" and unfamiliarity increase their attraction. The religious psychology of Carl Gustav Jung offers a key to understanding the unity and diversity among spiritual paths.

Many members of the Jewish tribe will say that this guidebook paints an unrepresentative portrait of the Jewish tradition, in that it overemphasizes some minor points and disregards some significant material. Unfortunately, since the Industrial Revolution, the spiritual side of Judaism has been in eclipse. Now the pendulum is beginning to swing back. This guide to Jewish spiritual growth is part of that back swing.

Membership in the Jewish tribe involves not only religion but all aspects of culture. Therefore, membership in the Jewish tribe is often described as a "way of life" rather than a "spiritual path." However, the *essence* of membership in the Jewish tribe is participation in the spiritual Way of Torah. The essence of the Way of Torah is the experience of the Oneness of God.

The current level of political, social and artistic activity within the Jewish world is extraordinarily high. However, not withstanding the recent rise of Orthodox fundamentalism, the current level of spiritual activity within the Jewish world is very low. Many people who are born into the Jewish tribe and who have strong spiritual hunger too often feel a need to seek their spiritual development elsewhere. In addition, few people who are comparison shopping for a spiritual path find the Jewish Way very inviting.

This spiritual guidebook hopes to lead you along the path to Jewish transformative experiences. Whether or not you were born a member of the Jewish tribe, it will explain *about* these experiences and invite you to try them out.

This book is interactive. Experiences are interspersed with explanations. To get the most out of this book, put it down and perform the experiences. To get the most out of the experiences, suspend some of your disbelief and your rational, critical mind for each experience's duration.

Do not label the results of any of these experiences "good" or "bad." Resist the inclination to say, "I couldn't do it right." The experiences are exactly that: experiences — things you do that have an effect on you. The journey is a process. Every point along the path is as "good" as any other point. Simply acknowledge and accept whatever an experience produces, without judgement. Have faith and trust that your experience will be a positive one.

You might want to acquire a special notebook. After each experience, take five minutes to record any important recollections or reflections. If time or place or your internal resistance make performing any of the experiences impossible, at least take a few moments and imagine what would happen if you did perform the experience.

Experience 1

Why are your reading this book?

1. Resolve to yourself that after you read the directions for this experience you will follow them.
2. Ask yourself, Why am I reading this book?
3. Answer yourself with whatever answer seems appropriate. Write your answer down in your notebook.
4. Ask yourself again, Why am I reading this book?
5. Answer yourself again. Your second answer can be the same as your first, or it can be different. Whatever answer comes up from within you is acceptable. Record this answer.

6. Continue asking and answering this same question for ten minutes. Record all answers, even the ones which seem unimportant.
7. Compare your first answer with your last.

❖

This Jewish spiritual guidebook has a goal: to give you the opportunity to move closer to the ultimate Jewish spiritual experience, the experience of the Oneness of God.

With God's help you will be successful.

Chapter 1

Freud and Jung and Their Jewish Connection

Whether God is real or illusion, the *experience of* God is real. The world's spiritual literature describes the power of the experience of God upon individuals who have had it. The continuing presence of spiritual activity in every culture and country of the world's history indicates that spiritual experience is an intrinsic aspect of human nature.

Spiritual experience is perceived as the embodiment of change and transformation. Nowadays, in the West, the study of processes of change belongs to psychology. Therefore, at least on one level, a spiritual path is a psychological process which we can study. Sometimes learning about an experience is a prelude to actually having the experience.

Specifically, the work of Carl Gustav Jung (1875-1961), as well as the story of his relationship with his mentor Sigmund Freud (1856-1939) provide an important theoretical foundation to understanding the Jewish spiritual path.

The essential premise of modern psychology is that deep within the psyche lie memories, feelings and drives of which we are not conscious. These unconscious processes effect everything we do, despite our conscious goals or desires.

Modern psychology began with Sigmund Freud, who believed that the growth of science would render religion obsolete. In

1

1927, in *The Future Of An Illusion*,[1] Freud argued that
religion, while an essential force in the development of civilization, had been created by the rational mind in order to bridle
otherwise untamable instincts toward sex and violence. Religious
teachings were accepted, he argued, because they claimed to
originate from God.

According to Freud, the idea of God was itself a projection
of the human mind. As infants, each individual trusts and experiences the love and protection of the father. As adults, each
individual imagines a celestial father who loves and protects in
the same way. Without this formulation of God, we would
forever feel ourselves to be at nature's mercy.

Freud wrote that since the Age of Science had dawned, hu-
mankind was ready to outgrow its childish need for religion.
Science would now explain once awesome natural events. Science
would even explain things for which religion claimed special revelation. According to Freud, religion was an illusion on the brink
of death.

Freud's last book, *Moses and Monotheism*[2] written in 1939,
attempted to debunk the Torah's account of the origins of Judaism. According to Freud, Moses was an Egyptian prince whose
"baby in the bullrushes" story was fabricated to ascribe to him
a Hebrew ancestry. Moses traded his palace for the leadership
of a band of slaves, to whom he taught devotion to an unseen
God in the wilderness. Before long, the slaves grew resentful of
this demanding God and killed Moses, God's spokesperson. Consumed with guilt over their crime, they elevated Moses to his
exalted role in history and became even more devoted to his God.
Thus, in Freud's account, the ancient Hebrews acted out the drama of Oedipus, killing their father to be free of his tyranny and
then were forever enslaved by their guilt.

Although Freud did not embrace traditional religious beliefs,

---

[1] Freud, S. *The Future of An Illusion*. 1927.
[2] Freud, S. *Moses and Monotheism*. 1939.

he was born a Jew and identified strongly as a Jew from an ethnic and sociological perspective. In 1926, Freud wrote a now-
famous letter to the Vienna Society of B'nai B'rith, an international Jewish men's fraternal and benevolent society. Freud
lamented that while his radical theories had made him an out-
cast in the medical world, his association with B'nai B'rith gave
him acceptance by a circle of men of high character. Freud went
on to say that his attraction to Jewry consisted of powerful, emotional forces that could not be expressed in words. He called it
"psychic bonding." Being a Jew, he added, helped prepare him
both to survive outside the majority and to face opposition.

In fact, Freud was haunted throughout his life by anti-
Semitism. He was acutely aware that many of his critics dismissed
his work simply because he was a Jew. Virtually all of his first
circle of students were Jews. However, when it came time to
choose a designated successor, Freud intentionally selected not
only a non-Jew, but the son of a Protestant minister, Carl Jung.

Ultimately, Jung found Freud overbearing and his theories too
narrow. The two men parted company. Jung went on to elaborate
a psychology of religion which has become essential to understanding religious experience: He maintained that this experience
is a natural, intrinsic part of the human life cycle. While Freud
is the father of modern psychology, Jung is the father of modern
psychology of religion. Any attempt to understand religion in
all its spiritual, scientific, psychological and theological aspects
begins with Jung.

However, his early writings reflect typical Christian misunder-
standings of Judaism; a few early statements appear anti-Semitic.
Later in life, he studied Jewish esoteric writings and he became
enthusiastic about their psychological significance and encouraged
their study.

Because of his early writings and also because Jung accepted
the chairmanship of the General Medical Society of Psychotherapy after the Nazis removed Jews from all German professional
societies, Jung has been accused of Nazi collaboration. He in-

sisted that he accepted the post in order to create an "international section" to which Jews could belong and thus continue practicing. While evidence clearly supports Jung's innocence, his anti-Semitism has remained a source of debate.

Thus, modern psychology begins with Sigmund Freud, a Jew by birth and social identification, with no use for any religion but sensitive to anti-Semitism. His chosen successor, Carl Jung, gave spiritual experience a new intellectual respectability, while he has been unfairly accused of anti-Semitism.[3]

Jung's Theories of the Collective Unconscious and the Archetypes

Jung realized that certain religious experiences and mythological patterns were common to all cultures throughout the world. He created a vocabulary to explain this phenomenon through his theories of the collective unconscious and archetypes.

Jung agreed with Freud that there was an unconscious part of the mind of each individual. This unconscious material expresses itself in dreams, neurotic symptoms, and in misunderstood actions and unacknowledged feelings. While Freud saw all unconscious activity rooted in childhood sexual instincts, Jung saw spiritual instincts — such as the drive to create beauty and harmony, to understand the meaning of human existence, or to live in altruistic service — as equally strong components of the unconscious.

According to Freud, an infant has an essential conflict between its instinctual drives for instant gratification — the *id* — and the controls imposed by culture — the *superego*. The major conflict of an infant is the well known Oedipal drama: the id wants sexual connection with the parent of the opposite sex; the superego says no. Anger and frustration result; the conflict must be resolved. The individual finally accepts its limitations, but the

---

[3]Kirsch, J. "Carl Gustav Jung and the Jews: The Real Story." *Journal of Psychology and Judaism*, Vol. 6 no. 2, Spring/Summer 1982, p. 113-143.

residual feelings of desire and frustration continue to work in the subconscious. Consequently, according to Freud, infant sexuality is the most basic element of all human activity and the drive which creates patterns of behavior throughout one's life.

Jung recognized that many elements of the unconscious are not rooted in the individual struggle of the child, as is the Oedipal drama, but are instinctual and common to all individuals. These elements arise from a deeper level of the human psyche which Jung called the collective unconscious.

Jung identified mythological motifs that have repeated themselves throughout the ages. For example, a wide range of cultures revere heroes who have miraculous births: Moses, Cyrus, Romulus, Oedipus, Paris, Heracles, Gilgamesh, Krishna, Jesus. Typically, the hero is born to nobles, his future foretold in a dream. He is raised by commoners or animals. As an adult he has great adventures and eventually learns of his true origin.

Freud maintained that this universal pattern was due to the actual experience of every child. The child is born believing in the father's great power (noble birth), only later to learn the father's limits (common birth). Jung argued that these common motifs are produced spontaneously by a "mythmaking" element in the unconscious, and that they are part of the shared unconscious material of all individuals.

While Freud had defined the personal unconscious, Jung continued to explore the collective unconscious. It is from this collective part of the psyche that archetypes emerge, figures and situations which repeat themselves across cultural and generational barriers. Furthermore, these archetypal situations and motifs manifest themselves in the stages of real life experience. The hero myths, while epic in nature, provide an outline for all human experience and behavior. The struggle to grow to maturity, for instance, or the will to face and overcome a great fear are the same elements portrayed in heroic mythology.

Jung identified a variety of archetypal figures: the divine child, the trickster, the "double," the wise old man, the primordial mother. These characters manifest themselves as "sub-personalities," or personifications of feelings, prompted by the unconscious. For example, each child's need for mothering gives rise to the experience of various goddesses, the personification of Mother Earth, the wicked stepmother, the fairy godmother, and the all-wise animal mother. These goddess figures within exert a tremendous influence on the individual's behavior.

The mythmaking function of the collective unconscious happens on three levels: personal, national and universal. On the personal level, we create our individual variations on the archetypes in response to our own unique set of life experiences. The personal unconscious—repressed memories, pains and fears, as well as unacknowledged perceptions—draws images from the collective unconscious and tailors them to create its conception of reality.

On the second level, the conception of reality is drawn from the unconscious material which is shared by family, social group, tribe, and nation. From birth, in subtle and not-so-subtle ways, we receive messages about the archetypes. The culture into which we are born is engraving images even before we can speak. Like photographic film which is exposed but undeveloped, archetypes are subject to manipulation in the darkroom. The central hero of the Torah is Moses. A Jew might not respond with equal emotional attachment to other variations on the great hero archetype, such as Krishna.

On the universal level of the collective unconscious we are all essentially alike, without personal or nationalistic distinctions. We all strive for high ideals, battle with demons, recognize higher powers. So while our experience of the archetypes is uniquely our own and it bears the indelible stamp of our culture, we also partake in the oneness of all individuals.

The Collective Unconscious and Being a Jew

To be human is to participate in the collective unconscious.

The existence of the collective unconscious and the archetypes implies that human beings are genetically predetermined to experience God. The drive to experience God is deep and unique, not simply fear of the unknown, or a projection or atavistic impulse. It cannot be reduced to lesser terms. The experience of God may remain dormant for years, even generations, but it is too much a part of our species to be forgotten or outgrown.

If you were born a Jew, the stories you learned as a child around the Passover *seder* or in Religious School were important factors in your development. As a result, your most significant religious experiences are most likely to have Jewish components.

Evidence suggests that at some level there is an archetypal awareness of one's heritage which is also passed down through the collective unconscious. Many converts to Judaism suddenly discover they have a Jewish relative during or just after their conversion. Similarly, there are people who are born Jews, but know nothing else about Judaism until one day Judaism unexpectedly becomes the predominant force in their lives. Whole communities, like the Jews in the Soviet Union, have suddenly awakened to the power of their dormant Jewish feelings.

Being born a Jew means being born with a certain history. Our lineage extends back 4000 years to the dawn of history. Beginning with Abraham and continuing through Moses, the Israelite Prophets, the Rabbis of the Talmud, the medieval philosophers and visionaries, down to the architects of modern Judaism, the one concern that gives meaning to life has been the experience of God.

These are the essential questions asked by each generation of Jews: "What has been our experience of God until now?" "How are things different now from what they have been?" "What must we do now to make the experience available to us?" The answers change, but the questions do not.

Jews display a range of attitudes toward the Jewish religion from loving embrace to vile disgust. However, it is impossible to "wish away" the contents of the unconscious. If you desire the experience God, and if you are born and raised a Jew, then you may be compelled to explore your Jewishness. If you attempt to grow in another spiritual tradition, you may eventually find yourself forced to confront the Jewish archetypes.

The Jew who goes to meditate in a Zen monastery, for instance, may discover the path is impeded not only by the difficulties of grasping Zen but by the sudden emergence of inherent Jewish material. When a Jew delves deeply into the unconscious while on a spiritual path, certain "Jewish questions" are bound to arise: "Why was I born a Jew?" "What have I learned from this 'accident'?" "What is the Jewish equivalent of Zen's *satori* (enlightenment)?"

Anyone can *learn about* the Jewish spiritual path. If your goal is to *experience* the Jewish path, but you are not born a Jew, then the tribal dimension of being a Jew may seem like an obstacle. However, as you pursue this process, you may discover that the Jewish archetypes resonate within you to such a degree that you are drawn farther along the path. In fact, the Jewish archetypes may already be waiting in your unconscious.

Spiritual growth means exploring ones innermost self to the deepest, most essential core. It means finding out who we are, why we were born, what we must learn in this lifetime and what tasks we must perform. The archetypes and the collective unconscious are concepts which are not likely to appeal to our rational faculties, until we experience them. Once experienced, these concepts become an unshakable part of the way we interpret our existence on this planet.

Experience 2

Meeting Your Archetypes

This exercise is best done by reading the following script into a tape recorder and then following its directions as you play it back to yourself. Or you can have a friend read it to you. In either case, it should be read slowly to give its images time to emerge from within.

Some of the later visualization experiences in this book will begin and end in the same manner as this one. If you have never done this kind of relaxation exercise, you will find that it gets easier as you go along and its effects will intensify. Remember to tell yourself that whatever images emerge in your mind are valuable. Don't minimize their significance by thinking that you just "made up that stuff." Whatever images come forth have been in your psyche for years, waiting to emerge.

Before You Begin:

Take your phone off the hook. Do whatever else you can to eliminate the possibility of being interrupted. Find a comfortable place to sit or lie down, undisturbed for about 30 minutes.

Dialogue to Be Heard:

Take a few very deep breaths. As you breathe allow your body to relax. Sink down into your chair or floor. Keep breathing deeply. Let your eyelids grow heavy. Feel your eyelids growing heavy and closing. Feel your whole body beginning to grow very relaxed now, growing deeper and deeper, very relaxed. Your eyelids are heavy now....heavier and heavier...[PAUSE 20 SECONDS].

Your entire body is relaxing now, mentally and physically from the top of your head all the way down to the very tips of your toes. You're growing relaxed, deeper and deeper. Relaxed and more relaxed. Now mentally scan your body from your toes up to your head and relax each part of your body. Tell each part of your body to relax. Relax your toes and your feet and your calves and your thighs and your stomach and inner organs. Relax your hands and your arms. Relax your shoulders and your lungs. Relax your neck and your face and your forehead and the muscles on top of your head. Now you are fully relaxed. Breathe deeply and follow the sound of my voice.

Visualize yourself standing in a corridor. It is a dimly lit corridor. You can barely see. It is a corridor that you know. You've been here before. It's a long corridor and along the corridor there are many doorways...One of the doorways looks more familiar to you than the others. It has a sign on it. It says: "Where the Wise One is." Open the door. You see it's dark inside but as your eyes adjust you see a dimly lit area in the far end of the room. There is a stool and seated on the stool is a Being of Great Wisdom. You can't tell yet if it's a man, woman, child or animal. Walk to the corner of the room and meet that Being. Introduce yourself in whatever manner seems appropriate. Let the Being respond to you. Ask the Being its name. Let the Being tell you something that it knows you need to know. [TAKE LONG PAUSE]

Acknowledge the Being for sharing this information with you. There is one question that is deeply within you that the Being will answer for you. Let this question emerge. [TAKE LONG PAUSE]

Now ask the Being your question. Listen to the Being's response. There is something you want from the Being. Let the one thing you want emerge from within you. [LONG PAUSE]

Tell the Being what you want from it. Let the one thing you need from the Being emerge from within you. [LONG PAUSE]

Now tell the Being what you need from it. The Being has a gift for you. Let the Being give you its gift. Acknowledge the gift and give the Being a gift in return. [LONG PAUSE]

Express to the Being how you feel about having the opportunity to meet it. [PAUSE]

You're about to depart, so if there's anything else to say, do it now. [LONG PAUSE]

If the Being has anything more to share, it will do so now. [LONG PAUSE]

You're going to depart from the Being now. Say any "Farewells" you need to make, and let the Being say its "Farewells" to you. Acknowledge the Being once more and then retrace your steps, back through the room to the doorway you entered. Go back into the corridor...

Now I'm going to count to ten and as I do you are going to transport yourself to your usual mode of awakening. When I reach ten you will be back in the place where you started. One, two...you are beginning to return, energized and awakened... three, four, feeling your limbs beginning to want to move again, five, six, start breathing deeply, sending energy throughout yourself, seven and you're almost back, eight, deep breath, nine, open your eyes, ten.

❖

Chapter 2

Torah: What It Is and What It Isn't

Judaism is the Way of Torah.

Torah is the spiritual tradition of Judaism and the Jewish path to the experience of God. Its literal meaning is "Teaching." Nonliteral meanings include "Tao", "oracle" "the Law of All Things" and "the Way It All Works." In common usage, Torah has several meanings.

"*The* Torah" refers to the first five books of the Bible, Genesis through Deuteronomy. According to Jewish tradition, these books are the Bible's most sacred part. Recorded by Moses on Mt. Sinai over three thousand years ago, they recount the history of the world from its creation to Abraham becoming the Jewish patriarch; the saga of Abraham and his family for four generations until they are transplanted in Egypt; where eventually their descendants are made slaves; until they are rescued by God through the leadership of Moses; and Moses leads them through the wilderness while receiving God's instructions for spiritual growth.

"The Torah" is also the first of the three sections of the Hebrew Bible. The others are the Book of the Prophets (*nevi'im*), which recounts Jewish history for about 800 years after the death of Moses; and the Writings (*ketuvim*), which contains additional inspirational teachings from those centuries. *Tanakh*, the acronym of Torah, *nevi'im* and *ketuvim*, is the Jewish name for what Christianity calls "The Old Testament."

"*A* Torah" refers to a Hebrew copy of "The Torah" written by hand on a parchment scroll, usually two or three feet high. These scrolls are the most revered objects in Judaism and have a prominent place in the synagogue service.

"The Written Torah" refers to "the Torah", the first five books of the Bible, as you would see them written in "a Torah" scroll or printed in any edition of the Bible.

"The Oral Torah" refers to all of the authoritative explanations of "the Written Torah." According to Jewish tradition, while God revealed "the Written Torah" to Moses at Mt. Sinai, God also gave him thousands of additional spoken words clarifying it. For example, the Written Torah forbids work on the Sabbath. What constitutes work and what does not? The Oral Torah includes a list of thirty-nine categories of activities which are specifically forbidden.

As centuries passed, these additional words were preserved orally until the Third Century of the Common Era, when they were collected and edited into a book known as the *Mishnah*. Like the Torah, the *Mishnah* has become a subject for study and debate. In addition, an extended commentary on the *Mishnah* was produced over the next four centuries and called the *Gemara*. The *Mishnah* and the *Gemara* together comprise the *Talmud*, which is the centerpiece of the Oral Torah.

"Torah" refers to all of these, as well as the entire body of traditional interpretations, discussions, commentaries, codifications and explanations of the Written Torah and the Oral Torah from ancient times to the present. "Torah" also indicates the dynamic, metaphysical process that produces this body of work.

Common Mistakes

Of all the world's great spiritual traditions, Torah is subject to the most misconceptions. Both Jews and non-Jews, admirers and detractors alike, make four common mistakes when describing Torah.

One frequent mistake is the basic Christian premise that "Torah equals law." The Christian scriptures account for this misunderstanding as they translate the word "Torah" as "Law." It is a mistranslation which colors the entire Christian perception of Torah and turns Torah into a litany of eight thousand "Thou shalt nots."

The Apostle Paul, whose writings form a large part of Christian Scriptures, explained that the Law (read "Torah") was a primitive instrument for attaining salvation which was superceded by faith in the divinity of Jesus. He wrote, "No human being can be judged righteous in the sight of God by observing the Law. All the Law can do is to make man conscious of sin" (ROMANS 3:20).

If "Torah" is substituted for "Law" in this passage, it becomes clear why the Christian Scriptures have created a negative reaction to the Path of Torah. This attitude has been ingrained in virtually all Christian writings for nearly two thousand years and continues to persist.

A second common misunderstanding is in taking only one of Torah's facets as its sum total. Sometimes Torah is seen as a guide to moral and ethical conduct, sometimes as a political document or history or philosophy or anthropology text. This kind of categorization diverts attention from the fact that Torah is the Jewish path to the experience of God.

Morals and ethics are certainly one of Torah's primary concerns. The climax of the Torah was the moment when The Ten Commandments were pronounced and the ethical-moral basis of Jewish culture established. One of the Torah's central themes is that the general principles of justice (*mishpat*) and rightness (*zedek*) are the foundation stones of life. The Torah is filled with the minute details of how to put these principles into action.

The Torah was also the political constitution of the ancient Israeli state. It is the oldest known political document to place the monarchy under the rule of a higher law. In addition, Torah records the history of Israel from its first ancestor, Abraham, through the death of Moses. Some of the material is legendary, but it contains enough fact that an authentic reconstruction of ancient history can be derived from it.

The Torah is an early philosophic text. Torah maintains that God is the first cause of everything that occurs on this earth, that God created the world out of nothing, that the world has purpose and order and that God's will to humans becomes known at certain moments.

Torah is also one of anthropological treasure troves of the world's religious literature. It contains mythology of the creation of the world, complete with paradise, serpents, floods. It includes sagas of patriarchs and matriarchs, complete with elaborate details of their families, lives, dreams and rituals.

The Torah can be a textbook in each of these categories. But Torah is more than the sum total of its parts.

Experience 3

Different Levels of Torah

Obtain a copy of the Torah in English. You can use any Bible edition you have, however the New Jewish Publications Society[1] translation is recommended.

Open it at random to any page. Read that page as if it were a guide to moral conduct and nothing more.

Read that same page again as though it were a political document, nothing more.

Continue reading it as a history text, a philosophy text, an anthropological document.

Read it once more and ask yourself, "What else can this page

---

[1] *The Torah*. Philadelphia: Jewish Publications Society, 1962.

of the Torah be?" Reflect or meditate on this question for several minutes. Write down whatever answers emerge.

❖

A third common error in evaluating the Torah is a fundamentalist mistake. Some passages in the Torah sound primitive and bloodthirsty to our modern ears, as well as chauvanistic, unforgiving, unrealistic. The Torah mandates death penalties for relatively minor infractions, such as gathering food on the Sabbath. The ancient Israelites were told to annihilate the Canaanite nations which they dispossessed.

Biblical fundamentalism assumes that these stories and lessons are to be interpreted according to the plain meaning of the Written Torah. However, in Jewish tradition the Torah is not meant to be taken literally without first consulting the Oral Torah and the interpretations of the Rabbis. The well known injunction of "an eye for an eye, a tooth for a tooth" (EXODUS 21:23) implies one should exact revenge. This verse is frequently cited as evidence of the compulsive and primitive legalism of Torah. In fact, the Talmud understands this law to mean that for the loss of an eye the victim is entitled to just monetary compensation (B. BABA KAMA 83B-84A).[2] Although the death penalty is specified in the Written Torah for a variety of crimes, the *Mishnah* notes that "a court that puts a man to death once in seven years is called a murderous one" (M. MAKOT 1:10).

Ironically, the Rabbinic understanding of problems in the Torah's text often generates a fundamentalism of its own. Rabbinic fundamentalism picks one particular way which the Oral

---

[2]Talmudic citations from the *Mishnah* are conventianally listed as "M." for *Mishnah*, followed by the tractate name and chapter and verse numbers. Citations from the *Gemara* are listed as "B." for "Babylonian Gemara" or "J." for "Jerusalem Gemara," followed by the folio pagination of the Standard, Vilna Edition.

Torah suggests and elevates it to a position of sole authority. One of the most perplexing incidents in the saga of Abraham comes when, after Abraham has been childless until old age, God commands him to offer his son as a sacrifice (GENESIS 22). The Torah's text implies that his son, Isaac, was a young child at the time. The predominant Rabbinic interpretation maintains that Isaac was thirty-seven years old. The thrust of the incident changes radically if the son is a mature adult.

Since struggling with the myths of the Torah is a central part of travelling the spiritual path, any literal or fundamentalist approach takes away from both the excitement and purpose of the struggle.

Finally, the fourth mistake which obscures Torah's nature is academic reductionism. This is the "explaining away" of the unique or extraordinary stories in the Torah, usually by means of scientific arguments. For example, the Torah tells that a series of ten plagues were visited upon the Egyptians in order to persuade them to release the Israelite slaves. No where in any ancient Egyptian text which has come to light is there mention of anything regarding these plagues. Reductionists use this as proof that the plagues did not occur. Whether or not they did occur misses the point of the story.

A variation of reductionism is the cutting and repasting of the Torah into different configurations to reconstruct the original pieces from which the Torah was first created. If a story is repeated in the Torah, reductionists conclude that it's two versions of the same story are only repeated due to faulty editing. Applying superficial contemporary literary standards to the Torah ignores its greatest depth and subtleties.

Academic reductionists also believe that transmission of the Torah through the ages has been careless and that its ambiguous lines or lapses in grammar must be corrected to say something else. Again, this approach imposes contemporary literary standards on an ancient text and eliminates the valuable tension of struggling with its deeper meanings.

Torah Is a Spiritual Text

A spiritual text teaches a variety of different lessons, often simultaneously. The most important level is also the most difficult one and even requires a certain suspension of disbelief. Looking at the Torah as a spiritual text does not come easily to children of a rational generation. Seeing the Torah this way leads the viewer into an unfamiliar region. It is a realm which feels unconnected from the known world, one that has been carefully cultivated according to personal desires and goals.

It may be easier to understand the Torah if we look at spiritual texts in general. A spiritual text is a map. A map is a symbolic representation of something much larger than itself, and something which helps us to get from one place to another.

As such, a spiritual text is a map of the psyche, a guide to those parts of a human being which are not immediately obvious. The highest, most evolved part of the soul, is the Higher Self or *neshamah*. A spiritual text is a guide to the relationship of your innermost core, your Higher Self, to the entire universe.

Each of us begins life as a single cell which then grows through a series of clearly defined life stages from embryo to maturity. Likewise, we grow emotionally, experiencing a range of feelings from love to hate, pleasure to pain. We also grow mentally and learn to perform a wide variety of intellectual tasks. For each of these types of growth there are teachers and texts to identify and assist in the process.

However, there is another type of human development: the growth of the spirit. The hallmarks of this process are twofold. The first is becoming aware that all events in the universe are manifestations of one essential unity and that they proceed with logic and harmony, even when the pattern is hard to perceive. The second is uncovering the depths of what is within ourselves: our powers to control and discern the world around us, as well as accept those aspects which are beyond our control. It is not a simple process, but one that demands work, pain, risk and reward. Growth of the spirit proceeds, not through being "taught about," but through our own personal experience. Spiritual texts like the Torah are guides to this growth.

The *Bhagavad Gita*

One of the most revered books in the world is the *Bhagavad Gita*, a Hindu classic. It begins with the tale of Arjuna, a warrior who nervously awaits a major battle. His fear is compounded by the fact that among the enemy's warriors are his brothers, parents, teachers and erstwhile friends. Whether he wins or loses, he will suffer greatly. Arjuna's charioteer is Krishna, who unknown to him is an incarnation of the god Vishnu, the Almighty Preserver of the Universe. As the battle draws near they engage in dialogue.

On a simple level, their conversation is about a god revealing the truth to a mortal. Krishna explains to Arjuna that all his emotional ties are now obstacles which must be understood differently if Arjuna is to grasp the truth. Salvation, continues Krishna, comes from either renunciation of the world (*samkhya*) or through selfless action (*karmayoga*), the latter being far simpler. The central task of each individual is to act in harmony with his or her higher destiny. All events that unfold are part of the Divine design. Arjuna's task is to act his destiny as a warrior, to fulfill his purpose on earth in spite of his misgivings. As Arjuna comprehends Krishna's words, he experiences God most deeply. He is transformed and his fears abate.

On a another level, Krishna is the Higher Self. He is the God within, the counsellor and the wise friend, who does not engage in the struggle with the externals but holds the reins of the chariot and guides Arjuna according to his own inner direction.

The *Bhagavad Gita* is an inner dialogue between the everyday conscious personality and a hidden, inner part of the self which already knows the highest spiritual truths. The interpreters of the *Bhagavad Gita* perceive that this metaphysical knowledge is something with which we are born. In Jungian terms, it resides in the collective unconscious until it emerges into consciousness where it manifests as instructions from a higher source.

Experience 4

Reading a Spiritual Text

Obtain a copy of the *Bhagavad Gita*. (If you have a choice of translations, choose the one that is easiest to understand and not made difficult with flowery English or stilted rhyme.)

Read the first two chapters, interpreting the dialogue as spoken by a mortal and God.

Reread the chapters interpreting the dialogue as that between the conscious part of the individual and the hidden source of highest wisdom within that individual.

Spend a few moments reflecting or meditating on the difference between reading the text in these different ways.

❖

How the Torah Is Like the *Bhagavad Gita*

Similarly, the Torah is a saga that tells the story of the people of Israel. Along the way, God reveals the path of *mizvot*, the rituals and ethics which lead to the prosperity of the nation.

On the metaphysical level, the Torah is mythology. Its characters are Everyperson. The stories invite us to examine the characters as parts of our own psychic development. Like the *Bhagavad*

Gita, the Torah is a dialogue between the outer personality and the *neshamah*, the Higher Self within.

The *I Ching*

Another treasured spiritual text is the ancient Chinese oracle, the *I Ching*. An oracle assumes that there is an order in the cosmos. Events are not random, but happen with divine guidance. The *I Ching* translates this order into a series of sixty-four hexagrams. Each hexagram symbolizes an attribute of life and together in various combinations they provide a map to any life situation which may arise.

The *I Ching* maintains that the good life is achieved by the archetypal "Superior Man" when he develops his conscious awareness of the twin cosmic forces of *yin* and *yang*, the harmonious opposites of dynamic change which determine every life process. *Yin* and *yang* act in accordance with fixed laws which can be described by the hexagrams. To consult the *I Ching*, one flips a coin or draws straws to determine which hexagram is operative at the moment. The hexagram points to a corresponding poem which describes the direction of change. The Superior Man does not "follow the oracle's advice" or "submit to its powers" but rather he listens to its guidelines about the flow of events.

To the Western scientific mind the *I Ching* may sound silly. However, nearly everyone who approaches this oracle, even if filled with doubt, soon discovers that it works. We can "explain away" its amazing accuracy by judging the poems conveniently ambiguous—simply prodding our unconscious to make the evaluation. If we're anxious, the poem will appear as a warning; if confident, the poem will reinforce our confidence.

This explanation may be correct as far as it goes, but it doesn't acknowledge the depths of an oracle's functioning. The *I Ching* oracle comes from the collective unconscious and therefore our innermost core resonates with it. Our conscious fears or convictions are the top layer of our feelings, undergirded by the Higher

Self's greater awareness. The hexagrams of the *I Ching* are a direct route to this deeper place within us.

The most puzzling aspect of the *I Ching* is its connection to a random event. the toss of a coin, the drawing of a straw. Jung discussed this problem, and it led him to formulate the "synchronicity principle": We must assume that seemingly random events are governed by some greater principle or design, particularly when those random events include an apparent coincidence which defies all reasonable explanations based on coincidence alone.

Experience 5

Consulting the *I Ching*

Obtain a copy of the *I Ching*. Most editions have an introduction with directions on how to determine the appropriate hexagram to your question.

If you have doubts about the accuracy of the *I Ching*, tell yourself you will suspend these doubts for the next hour. Commit yourself to doing this exercise assured that the text is a powerful tool for obtaining knowledge.

Find a quiet, undisturbed place. Select a question which can be answered "yes" or "no", and to which you truly do not have an answer. Silently focus on the question for several minutes.

Consult the *I Ching* for the appropriate hexagram.

Focus your attention on the message it gives you until its deeper meaning becomes clear to you.

❖

How the Torah Is Like the *I Ching*

Like the *I Ching*, the Torah is an oracle. It's divided into small
sections each called a *sidrah*, and each week of the year has a
sidrah assigned to it. Every synagogue in the world reads the same
sidrah each week. The *sidrahs* correspond to the hexagrams of
the *I Ching* in that they are generated from the collective unconscious of the Jewish people. Therefore, the weekly *sidrah* offers
relevant counsel to the questions you might have at that time.

The *Bardo Thodal*

The *Bardo Thodol* or *The Tibetan Book of the Dead* is yet
another important spiritual text, though less well known or in-
ternationally revered as the *Bhagavad Gita* or *I Ching*. The *Bardo
Thodol* describes the stages of disintegration and transformation
that occur as a person dies. It describes the psychic happenings
at the moment of death, the dream-state which follows, and the
subsequent onset of the birth instinct that precedes rebirth into
a new incarnation. Through its description of reality and directions for spiritual growth, it facilitates our experiencing the stages
that the dying go through. Thus, it is one of the world's most
developed guides to alternative states of consciousness.

Although we spend most of our lifetime in one particular state
of consciousness, it is not the only one available to us. Most of
us are familiar with the dream state. Certain drugs can also bring
on alternative states. When the dream is over or the drugs worn
off, the Western tendency is to diminish the value of the experience. The Eastern tendency is to see the alternative experience
as reality and our normal state as inferior. The Hindu and Buddhist traditions have highly evolved systems of meditation which
facilitate experiences beyond the ordinary state of consciousness.

Experience 6

Remembering a Dream

Tell yourself that tomorrow morning when you wake up, you're going to remember one of your dreams. Even if you think you never dream, or never remember your dreams, you'll remember one within the next three mornings.

Between now and when you go to sleep, keep reminding yourself, "I'm going to have a dream that I'm going to remember." This simple declaration repeated to yourself several times is a sufficient aid.

Have a pad and pen on your nightstand (or a tape recorder with a blank tape loaded). Tell yourself that the minute you wake up, the first thing you'll do is write down or dictate everything you recall about what you were dreaming.

Upon awakening, write or dictate your dream IMMEDIATE-LY. If you wait even five minutes you'll forget it.

Later in the day, read or play back what you've put down. Recall the images, and how you felt during the dream.

Ask yourself, "How do I know I'm not dreaming now?"

❖

How the Torah Is Like the *Bardo Thodal*

Like all the world's great spiritual texts, the Torah is also a guide to alternative states of consciousness. The conversations of Abraham, Jacob, Moses and others with God are paradigms of alternative states of consciousness where higher knowledge is available. Using Torah as a spiritual text requires opening yourself to its power, which means opening yourself to alternative states of consciousness.

Chapter 3

Aggaadah — Torahitic Mythology

The Torah is a guide to the psyche, an oracle and a map of alternative states of consciousness. As spiritual text, Torah works through two specific modalities: *aggadah* and *halakhah*.

Aggadah (or *midrash*) is a process of reading the text to understand Torah's mythos, metaphysics and archetypes. *Halakhah*, "the proper performance of *mizvot*," is a process of correct actions that facilitates spiritual experience.

Metaphysical Midrash

Mythology is a reflection of the soul. What each culture feels most deeply it casts into its myths. Therefore, mythologizing is the process of casting inner experience into fables. Torah unfolds a mythic tale. In its encoded language, the myth gives us information that transforms our meaningless physical existence into a piece of the grand design animating the whole universe. Through the Torah's myth we learn metaphysics and the Jewish archetypes.

Metaphysics asks the essential question, "What in the universe is real?" The concept is so basic as to be easily overlooked. It inspires other questions, such as, "Why is the physical world here?" "How did I get here?" "Do I have a purpose in life?"

Jewish archetypes are models of the process of spiritual growth. They offer us examples of people who have become aware of such questions, and wrestled with them. The Jewish archetypes are also metaphors for the soul itself as it grows and flows through each moment in time, often with great difficulty.

Aggadah means "something to tell" as in "to tell a tale." *Midrash* means "inquiry." The terms are more or less synonymous. *Midrash* is a process of probing the Torah's tales to learn the depth of its insights. To engage in *midrash* is likened to wrestling with God. The name Israel means "God-wrestler." *Aggadah* is the *sine qua non* of Judaism. Without wrestling with God, Judaism is impossible. Therefore, to engage in *midrash* is essential to the Jewish spiritual path.

There are volumes of ancient *midrash* which offer dozens of completely different interpretations for a single line in the Torah's text. Each interpretation is correct within its context. *Aggadah* makes no effort to be consistent. Whichever lines of *midrash* resonate in your soul are the only "correct" ones.

Creation

The Torah's familiar recounting of creation and expulsion from paradise imply a metaphysics by employing archetypal symbols. The universe emanates from, and is inextricably a part of, God-Who-Is-One.

The Torah contains two recountings of creation. The first creation story (GENESIS 1:1-2:4) is linear, technological, and orderly. Creation begins with Primordial Light, and simple structures and creatures precede the more complex. The second creation story (GENESIS 2:4-24) is dreamlike, intuitive, primeval. Everything suddenly arises fullblown with the primordial Paradise. In one story, man and woman are created together as equals (GENESIS 1:27). In the other, woman is created out of man (GENESIS 2:22). Torah's originality among world mythologies emerges by telling the story from both perspectives and placing them unapologetically side by side. The Torah's subtlety mirrors the ambiguity of human experience.

In Torah's mythology, the primordial Earthling (*Adam*) is created by God, not identified with God. He and Earth Mother (*Ḥavvah*) are created neither good nor evil, but with the opposing inclinations towards both. They participate with God in creation as they give things names (GENESIS 2:19). The Garden of Delights (*Eden*) is their pre-conscious state which the Primeval Serpent Uroboros (*Naḥash*), the impregnating self-awareness, intrudes upon them. Humans become "godlike" (GENESIS 3:22). The expulsion from Paradise is the birth of consciousness and the opportunity to begin the journey to transcendence.

Archetypal Ancestors

From the Creation of the world, the Torah charts the spreading out of people across the face of the earth until it focuses upon its central area of concern: the line of Abraham. The story then shifts from metaphysics to archetypal human characters enacting mythological dramas. The Torah gives us "spiritual biographies," life stories of the Founding Giants to remind us that whatever crisis we encounter, they have been encountered before.

Experience 7

Remembering Torah's Archetypes

Some of the Torah's tales may not be familiar to you. Read the rest of this chapter with a copy of the Torah at hand (again any edition of The Bible will do). Look up any of the references to stories or incidents you don't know or recall.

❖

The Ten Trials of Abraham

The spiritual biography of Abraham focuses on his quality of compassion and on his ten trials (M. Avot 5:4). Abraham was the embodiment of compassion (*ḥesed*). When strangers came to his tent he treated them as honored guests (Genesis 18:1-5). Even when God angrily threatened to destroy two cities, Abraham took the role of counsellor to God, teaching infinite compassion, even to God (Genesis 18:20).

Abraham's series of trials begins when, in his maturity, he suddenly intuits the Oneness of God. God responds by instructing him to leave his ancestral home (Genesis 12:1). He follows God's promise for a good life in Canaan, only to have a famine force him to move to Egypt (Genesis 12:10). He heeds his wife Sarah's insistence that he drive away his concubine Hagar and his son by her, Ishmael (Genesis 12:10), and then he stands by helplessly as Sarah is abducted into the palaces of Pharaoh (Genesis 12:15) and later of Abimelech (Genesis 20:2). He courageously goes to war (Genesis 14:14). In his eighth trial, he learns from God that his descendants would be enslaved for four hundred years (Genesis 15:7). In the ninth trial, God commands him, by then a very old man, to circumcise himself (Genesis 17:9).

Abraham's last trial is one of the Torah's dramatic climaxes. God had promised Abraham that he would be ancestor to a great nation, but Abraham and Sarah are old and remain childless. Then Isaac is born. God's promise seems possible until God tells Abraham to take his son and sacrifice him on a mountain top in the Land of Moriah (Genesis 22:2). Abraham obeys, and at the last moment Isaac is spared. Being prepared to give up all one has acquired and trusting that everything that occurs is a manifestation of God's will is the essence of spiritual perfection. Abraham's own agony does not deter him from meeting the challenge of his greatest trial. Abraham's experience of God overpowers even his own will for his progeny to survive.

The Stories of Isaac and Jacob

While the archetype of Abraham teaches compassion and trust, (*emunah*) the archetype of Isaac teaches strength (*gevurah*) and fear of God (*paḥad*). Compared to Abraham, his life story is simple, consistent and undramatic. He worked hard, set standards of perfection for himself and carried them out. Most individuals live a large part of their lives under the sign of Isaac.

Isaac has twin sons. The first born Esau, and second born Jacob. Jacob's archetype, "splendid splendor" (*tiferet*) and truth (*emet*), is a synthesis of his father and his grandfather. Compassion can become indulgent, strength can stifle achievement. Truth mediates between them.

Jacob's tale is continually riddled with deception, but in each case the will of God becomes clear in the unfolding of his destiny. His story begins with a lie: He tricks his father out of his brother Esau's blessing, then must run for his life to escape his brother's anger. Then his first night on the road he has a dream in which he learns that God's special providence guides his life (GENESIS 28:11). He travels to his uncle Laban's house where he falls in love with Rachel, but his uncle tricks him into marrying Leah first and Rachel only later (GENESIS 29:15ff). Again the truth unfolds, for both women were destined to become matriarchs of Israel.

Jacob makes a bargain with Laban for wages and prospers honestly from his skill. But Laban becomes threatened. Jacob must deceive him and flee (GENESIS 31:1ff). Truth unfolds again when the two make a treaty (GENESIS 31:43).

When Jacob is about to re-encounter his brother, he dreams again. "He is left all alone and someone wrestled with him until dawn" (GENESIS 3225). He wrestles with this adversary or angel or aspect of himself, until he is finally blessed with the name Israel, "God-wrestler." Thus, the name Israel refers to that part of the individual which struggles to comprehend the ultimate meaning of human experience. This wrestling match left Jacob with an archetypal, permanent injury, a limp that never heals.

Once again, his story reveals that wrestling with God must precede wisdom or truth.

Joseph the Dreamer

Jacob's struggle continues into the next generation. Of his twelve sons, the favorite is Joseph, who is gifted with precognitive dreams. Joseph dreams that one day his family will bow down before him. Jacob fears this dream while Joseph's brothers become very jealous of him (GENESIS 381ff). The brothers sell Joseph into slavery and Jacob believes him to be dead.

Joseph's ability as a dream interpreter elevates him to power (GENESIS 40:1ff). He later has an opportunity to test his now remorseful brothers before forgiving them (GENESIS 42-45). Joseph realizes that like his father and grandfathers before him, his brothers' evil intentions are part of God's plan to bring about a higher good (GENESIS 50:14).

The Feminine In the *Midrash* and the Four Matriarchs

The Torah has feminine elements, but we must probe deeply to recognize them in this male dominated text. The female characters have simply not been as developed by the events told in the Torah's myths. However, the female characters in the Torah, particularly the four matriarchs, are active, perceptive characters whose wills often override their husbands', and whose sense of God's is often far clearer. Just as the *I Ching* maintains that the entire workings of the universe result from the harmonious interaction of *yin* and *yang*, female and male energy, earth and heaven, so the Torah's archetypes balance their emphasis on *yang* archetypes with *yin* energy.

Abraham's wife, Sarah, is the first to realize that her handmaiden, Hagar, must leave (GENESIS 21). Rebecca is the first to know that Jacob is the favored grandson (GENESIS 27). Rachel transfers her father's spiritual power to her husband Jacob

(GENESIS 31:19-35). Each of these women mirrors her husband's central quality — compassion, strength, mediation — but in a form that is *yin*.

Sarah is a spiritual woman, filled with compassion. Her hearth epitomizes abundance and comfort (MIDRASH BERESHIT RABBAH 60:16). Her personal charisma is such that twice monarchs abduct her. Her husband's ten trials are condensed into one: her limitless compassion is coupled with barrenness. It puts severe strain on her marriage, destroys her relationship with Hagar, and even jeopardizes Hagar and her son (GENESIS 16, 21). Ultimately, her empathy is her demise. When she learns that her only son Isaac has nearly been sacrificed by her husband, she dies from shock (GENESIS 23:1).

Isaac's wife, Rebecca, manifests strength. When Rebecca enters the tribe, the feminine balance and perfection that was lost since Sarah's death is reestablished (GENESIS 24:67). She too is nearly abducted (GENESIS 26:6ff) and like Sarah she has trouble getting pregnant. An oracle tells her she will have twins whose battle has already begun (GENESIS 25:19f). This knowledge later gives her the strength to urge Jacob to deceive his father (GENESIS 27:5) and flee his brother (GENESIS 27:43).

Jacob's two wives are sisters, Rachel and Leah. Jacob marries Leah, his first wife, without desiring to do so (GENESIS 29:21f). A compassionate woman ("soft eyed" — GENESIS 29:17), she bears numerous children. Although she embodies the "eternal feminine," her sister Rachel is the more beloved. This is a reminder that men are generally more attracted to their own anima projections than to ultimate feminine power." Rachel is ephemeral, elusive, always longed for but out of reach (GENESIS 29). She is totally desirable, physically and spiritually, what Jung called an *anima* figure. She is Jacob's first love, but he must work fourteen years to wed her. She has difficulty becoming pregnant and dies while giving birth to her second child. She knows her destiny even as a young girl and is instrumental in facilitating the spiritual power of the men around her (GENESIS 31:14f).

The Exodus from Egypt

The experience of the Exodus is the Torah's central myth. It was such a powerful component in the Israelite national consciousness that it has determined all Jewish life ever since. On one level, the story of the national deliverance of the enslaved people is a metaphor for the evolutionary development of each individual, the one who wrestles with God within. At the festival of *Pesaḥ*, which commemorates the Exodus, the liturgy declares that, "In every generation, each individual is obligated to see oneself as if he or she had personally gone out of Egypt."

The Hebrew name for the Exodus is *"yeziat miẓrayim,"* which is usually translated "the going out of Egypt." It also implies "the letting go of Egypt." *Mitzraim*, Egypt, also connotes "narrowness." On the national level, the struggle is to leave the country. On the personal level, the struggle is to let go and leave behind the attachments to people, places and situations which have outlived their usefulness.

Letting go of attachments is difficult. The basic premise of Buddhism is that all life is suffering, caused by attachments, but that the suffering can be ended through the discipline of the Buddha's Eight-fold Path. Judaism does not concur that all life is suffering, but the Exodus myth agrees that we cling to what we have, even if it has lost its value and causes us to suffer. For instance, victims of physical family abuse, whether children or spouses, often struggle to keep a painful relationship intact. The security of regular paychecks can override the frustration of an unrewarding job. The end of a marriage is regarded as a tragic event in our culture, even if the marriage was destructive.

The Exodus story begins in Goshen, the place where Joseph's family settled when they arrived in Egypt. *Goshen* "*midrashes*" (i.e. "free associates") into the word *gooshah*, the soil, the substance of sustenance. This grounding is like the womb of Mother Earth: protecting, nurturing. *Goshen/Gooshah* is the security that allows life to continue. However, eventually comfort becomes constraint, safety becomes routine. The natural human urge for development bursts like a swelling seed.

On a mythological level, slavery represents the compulsion to direct energy in a particular manner. The Hebrew word for slave is *eved*, which has a dual connotation. An *eved* can be someone coerced into serving a human master, while an *eved YH*, a servant of God, is someone who serves God through free will. The divine spark within struggles to emerge. This transition of each individual is personified by the saga of the hero Moses.

Moses follows the archetypal journey of the hero: miraculous birth, a name expressing specialness ("I Drew Him Out"), a childhood in the palace, fall from power, exile and humble survival as shepherd for his father-in-law. Moses then stumbles in the Burning Bush and experiences God (Exodus 3:1). Suddenly he becomes aware of his higher destiny.

The God whom Moses experiences is formless. Naming anything is controlling it. God's name resists becoming too familiar. The name which God reveals to Moses, "I Am What I Am" (Exodus 3:14), implies a power that cannot be designated, much less controlled. This power is so strong that Moses cannot resist its demands. This name, "I Am" (Heb. *AHYH*), is linked etymologically to the unknowable, unpronounceable, most powerful of all God's names, *YHVH*. (When *YHVH* appears in print, we read *Adonai*, "My Lord.")

Pharaoh personifies resistance and ego-egocentricity in his unwillingness to give up his slaves. Change is difficult. We hesitate to give up our hard earned possessions. We continue to define ourselves according to the trappings of our outer existence—our things, our credentials, even our belief systems.

When Moses presses his demand, Pharaoh orders the slaves to work harder. The slaves then complain to Moses that he is only increasing their suffering. The pressure for change continues to build until the old system can no longer restrain its own growth.

Suddenly there is no more time to deliberate. The slaves must leave immediately, even before their bread can finish rising. We remember their haste when we celebrate *Pesaḥ* each year and eat unleavened bread. For three days they enjoy their newfound freedom, until they reach the Sea of Reeds or Red Sea. It is a terrible obstacle to overcome, and the ultimate moment of transition is in the last rush of being born.

Pharaoh mobilizes his forces and sends them to recapture his slaves, who are already complaining to Moses that they have been led into the desert only to die. Previous suffering is quickly forgotten. Moses urges them to let go of their fear and to trust in God. He raises his arms and makes the Sea turn into dry land for them to cross (EXODUS 14:21). As Pharaoh's charioteers pursue, Moses lowers his arms and the army is drowned. The people exalt and sing. They have been delivered from one stage of life to the next.

The Enlightenment of the Soul at Sinai

Sinai means both "mountain" and "ravine." The mountain rises up to touch the Heavens, while the ravine leads us into the deeper layers within. The two are one. Enlightenment involves knowing both the Beyond and the Within. Sinai is most often called "Revelation" rather than "Enlightenment." In fact, the two concepts are one. From God's point of view it is revelation; from the human perspective it is enlightenment. In either case, the acquisition of knowledge which resides in God is a joyful and transforming experience. Anxiety melts away. We sense that our life pattern bears perfect harmony, like a jigsaw puzzle thrown into the air whose pieces land into a perfect fit. But the moment is often short lived.

Only a few weeks after the slaves rejoice in their redemption, optimism fades. They fear starvation and they grumble against Moses (EXODUS 16:1f). Their faith in God is weak. God responds with food. Shortly after they make camp where there is no water. They complain; God responds with water. Just as the young adult outgrows his parent's protection but still struggles against internalized parental authority, so the liberated slaves remain slaves to their old, untrusting slave within.

Parts of the Soul

The Israelite nation's preparation for enlightenment is the paradigm of the path of the enlightenment of the soul. To truly understand this process, we must understand the definition of the soul according to Jewish tradition.

The soul has three essential parts: *nefesh, ru'aḥ* and *neshamah*. *Nefesh* includes the entire psycho-physical totality of humans, all the physical, emotional and rational components. *Ru'aḥ* represents an intermediate ethical level, the ability to distinguish between good and evil. *Neshamah* is the higher spiritual level, the Higher Self.

Before the world was created, God was truly One, infinite and everywhere, an undifferentiated unity. God then withdrew from a point within God's self to create the physical space of the universe. Like droplets from an ocean wave that separate from their Source for a brief moment, the *neshamah* begins and ends in God. Each *neshamah* is immortal. It knows its own destiny from before the moment it separated from God. It is a composite of male and female elements, and only in its descent does one side become dominant.

Ru'aḥ also originates in God, but its Divine essence has been further intertwined with the physical realities of this world. *Ru'aḥ* recognizes that there is good and evil, and that it has the power and obligation to choose between them.

At death, the *nefesh* remains in the grave, lamenting over the death of the body. The *ru'aḥ* ascends to whatever level of celestial paradise it has earned by the merits it has accrued, and the *neshamah* goes directly back to the fullness of God.

The Israelite's path of enlightenment combines *neshamah's* recognition of its origin and nature, with *ru'aḥ's* path of perfection. To reach enlightenment, the soul must declare itself ready—

ready to take a risk, to change, to wake up. Waking up requires
a willingness to experience the world differently. Moses gave his
people the option to accept a new state of consciousness. Their
unanimous response was, "All that God has said we will do!"
(EXODUS 19:8). Enlightenment carries a sense of urgency; once the
opportunity is glimpsed, it is impossible to ignore.

Amid thunder, lightning and blasts of the ram's horn, Moses
leads the people to the edge of the quaking, flaming mountain
(EXODUS 19:17). God descends; Moses ascends. This is dialogue.
The people must remain at a distance, at first because they are
warned (EXODUS 19:20), and then by choice (EXODUS 20:15f). They
recognize the danger that they may die if they gaze too closely.
In other words, the majority of the people are not ready for enlightenment. Their souls are still on the level of *nefesh*. They
resist enlightenment and are afraid of the mountain. The intensity of Moses' experience with God is absolutely unique, and yet
Moses is the archetype of growth toward God. The path up the
mountain lies before each of us.

The Ten Principles

God speaks and delivers the *Aseret ha-Dibbrot*, the Ten
Words, or the Ten Important Matters. They are principles, rather
than Commandments. Torah contains 613 Commandments
(*Miẓvot*). In fact, the first of the Ten Words is a statement: "I
Am, *YHYH*, your God, who brought you out of the land of
Egypt, the place of bondage" (EXODUS 20:1). The first word God
speaks to Moses is "*anokhee*," "I" (EXODUS 20:1). The power that
underlies the universe is an "I," an undifferentiated unity. God
is both the internal and external One. Recognizing their unity
is to experience life's greatest mystery.

"You shall have no other gods beside Me" (EXODUS 20:3) is the
Second Principle. Polytheism was the prevailing religion of the
times (and is still the alternative to God's Oneness). Here we
learn that *any* experience of God is a manifestation of the One

God. A glimpse of infinity in a lover's eyes isn't Aphrodite; a burst of powerful zeal isn't Mars. Both are experiences of the One God.

"You shall not make for yourself a sculptured image, nor bow down and serve them" (EXODUS 20: 4-5) is an amplification of the Second Principle. It is tempting to use a visual anchor to preserve the experience of God, but any one thing created by God, whether a person or the sun or the moon, is not God. Confusing God with God's creation minimalizes the vastness of the experience of God.

"You shall not take *YHVH* your God's name lightly" (EXODUS 20:7) teaches that even speaking the name of God invokes God's presence and makes God's power manifest. Invoking that power for a casual or impure purpose is a serious mistake. Once a person has progressed spiritually, he or she is empowered with the ability to sense things that others might miss. This is a power not to be misused.

"Remember the *Shabbat* and keep it holy" (EXODUS 20:8) reminds us that enlightenment demands a commitment — a special time set aside for spiritual work. *Shabbat* is one day in seven removed from the material world and all its seductive technology in order that we may fix our attention on God.

"Treat your father and your mother with great respect, in order that you live a long time on the land that *YHYH* your God is giving you" (EXODUS 20:12). Through the experience of being a child of earthly parents, we learn respect for the male and female archetypes. Our consciousness of maleness and femaleness is developed through our interaction with our parents. Furthermore, in a certain sense we select our particular parents because in this lifetime we have specific tasks to complete, lessons to learn. Our joys and pains with our parents are central to this work. The obstacles they impose upon us correlate with the qualities we must develop to overcome them. If the pain is still affecting our lives, then the lessons to be learned are still unfolding. Despite the problems our parents may cause us, we must respect them.

We selected them in order to fulfill our destiny.

These first five Important Principles are directed at the *neshamah* and are the keys to enlightenment. These *neshemah*-oriented principles are supplemented with the second five *ru'ah*-oriented principles, those concerned with actions and ethics. Each set is written on a separate tablet to indicate their complementary counterbalance. In spiritual work, there is always the danger of losing ones grounding in reality. There is the danger that the wonders of the inner journey will cause the seeker to neglect the responsibilities of the physical world. Judaism, more than any other tradition, is firmly rooted in this world. The quest for enlightenment is not license to ignore the importance of our community or family. However, these second five have an important level of significance to the *neshamah* as well.

"You shall not murder" (Exodus 20:13) indicates that protecting human life is the most basic prerequisite for ethical conduct. Human life is sacred. "Murder" (*rezah*) means "taking life needlessly" in Hebrew. Even in the most extreme circumstances, war and capital punishment, human life remains protected.

On the *neshamah* level, this Principle teaches us to increase our awareness to include respect for all life. As all life has its source in God, in the course of spiritual work you may feel compelled to extend this Principle to become a pacifist or vegetarian, to avoid leather and animal products, and to avoid killing even insects. While the *ru'ah* level does not demand it, the *neshamah* level may urge you to consider this response.

"You shall not commit adultery" (Exodus 20:13) is an injunction to respect the structure of the family and commitment to those relationships. On the *ru'ah* level, this instructs us to refuse sexual involvement with married individuals. Jewish culture has always regarded the nuclear family as a cornerstone of tribal continuity.

On the *neshamah* level, this Principle instructs us to reflect on our physical urges. Sexuality is a basic force in this world and is a factor in every human interaction. In many spiritual traditions, sexual energy is seen as the raw stuff which is transformed into spiritual energy. Many traditions (though Judaism is an exception in this regard) have an honored place for celibacy — not because sexuality is bad, but because spiritual growth requires increased awareness and direction of it.

"You shall not steal" (EXODUS 20:13) establishes rights of property. Ethical action demands respect for the essential fact that things belong to people. However, on the spiritual level, respect for property implies the importance of the physical world and this incarnation. Property is legitimate; the world and its things are important and our enjoyment of the world is important. The energy we expend to acquire things is good, as long as we devote energy to other pursuits as well. This may appear obvious, but most spiritual traditions denigrate the importance of possessions. The archetypal holy person is usually the homeless wanderer. However, the path to enlightenment through Torah does not suggest we divest ourselves of what we own, only that we acquire it honestly.

"You shall not bear false witness against your neighbor" (EXODUS 20:13) undergirds the strength of civilization by legitimizing its legal apparatus. Testimony in a court must be absolutely true and accurate. On a *neshamah* level, this Principle urges us to be mindful of every word we speak. Jewish tradition has always been aware of the power of *lashon hara*, speaking falsely or gossip. There is power in every word spoken. A single lie has the power to change a lifetime; a word blurted out in anger is apt to contain words that aren't true. We must be cautious with our every word, as though it were spoken as testimony in court.

"You shall not covet anything that is your neighbors" (EXODUS 20:14) is the final Principle. "Covet" (*hamad*) means not simply to "desire" something, but to become obsessed with it or to allow the desire to control you. Torah assigns no punishment for feelings which are not acted upon. Therefore, feelings of lust, hatred, desire and envy are acceptable. But desiring something so much it becomes an overwhelming preoccupation is more than mere feeling. It becomes an object with a life of its own.

On the *neshamah* level, this principle teaches that even our feelings can be brought under conscious control. By implication, no feeling can control our behavior unless we allow it to. Expanding awareness of our feelings keeps us conscious of their impact upon us. In limiting the power of random feelings, we gain access to the Higher Self.

In summary, on the spiritual level the Ten Principles tell us that 1) God is One, an "I"; 2) All experiences of God are experiences of this same One; 3) The power of God must be respected; 4) Spiritual work requires a commitment of time; 5) We chose our parents for an important reason.

On the ethical and spiritual level, the Principles tell us to 6) treasure all life; 7) to respect the spiritual potential in the physical body 8) to honor this world, in this place, in this incarnation; 9) to pay attention to our every word; 10) to rise above unexamined inclinations.

These principles are terribly demanding. Only days after accepting them, the people regress and build the Golden Calf (EXODUS 32:1f), an atavistic archetype of unrestrained physical gratification. Moses' dramatic return from the mountain, his smashing the tablets of these Ten Principles in a moments' unbridled anger, is a crashing cymbol to reawaken a newly emerged consciousness which has quickly returned to sleep.

The Promised Land and the Sense of the Ending

The spiritual journey now continues into the Promised Land.

After reaching enlightenment, the central task is to continue to live on this earth knowing one day we will die. Whether we believe there is an afterlife or resurrection or reincarnation — or nothing — accepting the reality of life's eventual end is life's most difficult task. The Torah presents this process in Moses' journey to the Promised Land.

The journey to the Promised Land continues as soon as the Israelites leave Sinai. For three days they march with the Ark of the Covenant, the emblem of God's leadership (NUMBERS 10:33). Soon the people begin to complain about life in the desert and question Moses' leadership. He laments to God that his role is too difficult for any one mortal to bear. Moses' cry is our first hint of his awareness of his own mortality.

Even Moses' own sister Miriam murmurs against him (NUMBERS 12:1f). Her negative energy manifests itself in her body as a serious skin disease and Moses prays for her: "Let her not be as a dead one, who emerges from his mother's womb with half his flesh eaten away" (NUMBERS 12:12). Moses has become aware of the fine line between life and death, and his anxiety is manifest in his prayer for her healing.

God instructs Moses to send spies ahead to explore the Promised Land (NUMBERS 13:1f). Twelve spies are dispatched. Ten return with disconcerting news: the land is inhabited by powerful people, the cities huge and fortified (NUMBERS 13:28). Two scouts return with a recommendation to immediately proceed to take possession of the land (NUMBERS 13:30). The people are frightened by the majority report and want to return to Egypt! God is ready to destroy the entire multitude and start over again with Moses alone, but Moses pleads for their lives. God's anger abates, but God declares that only the children of those who left Egypt will enter the Promised Land. With ominous foreshadowings, the sole exceptions mentioned are Joshua and Caleb, the two spies who advised moving forward.

Moses' next challenge comes when one of the people, Korah, launches an attack against his authority, charging him with assuming too much power (NUMBERS 16:3). Moses sets up a trial by ordeal, at the end of which the earth opens and swallows Korah and his supporters (NUMBERS 16:30). Moses is delivered from the latest challenge, but still the people question his authority. God responds by sending a devastating plague in which 15,000 people perish (NUMBERS 17:14).

Even though the story shows Moses overcoming one major crisis after another, he is human and his life is finite. This essential imperfection means that he will die before he reaches his last great goal, the Promised Land, even though by his actions he deserves to reach the Journey's completion.

The Hebrew sense of tragedy doesn't allow for fairytale conclusions. In Greek tragedy, the hero reaches the pinnacle of all human strivings, only to be cut down by forces he cannot control. Similarly, Moses meets every test that the people and God place before him. However, Moses' humanity makes some mistakes inevitable. One miniscule lapse is Moses' only concrete manifestation of his human imperfection. Because of this minor mistake, his goal unravels; his tragic flaw is his humanity.

After forty years in the desert, the Israelites are encamped at Kadesh (NUMBERS 20:1f). There is no water and the people are again ready to blame Moses for bringing them to the wilderness to die. Moses prays and God tells him to touch a rock with his staff. Moses does so, and only a trickle of water flows out. The people mock his ability to save them, at which point, according to the *Midrash* (BERESHIT RABBAH 191:19), Moses angrily smashes the rock with his staff and water flows. For this public display of anger, Moses is told he will not enter the Promised Land (NUMBERS 20:12; 27:14).

This tale implies that to travel the whole Journey from Egypt to Sinai to the Land of Israel is beyond human capabilities. In other words, the totality of one's work cannot be completed in a single lifetime.

According to tradition, Moses wrote every word of the five books of the Torah. The Talmud cites differing opinions, however, concerning the concluding verses which describe Moses' death. One sage says Joshua, Moses' successor, wrote them. Another says Moses himself wrote them with a tear in his eye while under prophetic inspiration (B.BABA BATRA 15a). Moses knew that his task was complete and he was ready to let go. He was allowed to glimpse the Promised Land from afar shortly before his death (DEUTERONOMY 34:1f). The dramatic poetry of this moment gives each individual an awareness of their own morality. In one sense, the only Promised Land is Death. The archetypal Journey of Moses is the Quest of Everyperson.

Experience 8

Writing Your Own *Midrash*

Read several sections about the other major archetypal institutions described in the Torah: the Priesthood, the Tabernacle or the Sacrifices (EXODUS 25-31, 35-40, LEVITICAS 1-10, 11-16, 21-22; 24:1-9, 27; NUMBERS 35, 6:22-10:28). Write an outline for your own understanding of these. You might start by considering:
—What is the psychic symbolism of the High Priest?
Consider the dedication of Aaron as High Priest (LEVITICUS 8), the High Priest's special ritual for *Yom Kippur* (LEVITICUS 16), the Priest's regulation not to come in contact with death (LEVITICUS 21) and the Priest's vestments (EXODUS 28).
—What are the types of sacrifices described in Leviticus 1-7? What activities might have required these types of sacrifices? What emotions would be aroused by the act of watching an animal killed and offered to God?
—Read the "blueprints of the Tabernacle" (EXODUS 25-27) and imagine it exactly as it looked. Close your eyes and construct each piece of it in your mind. When completed, imagine yourself entering it and notice the experience.

❖

The Emergence of the Soul

The *neshamah*, the Higher Self, becomes conscious of itself through an unfolding process. Since birth, this all-knowing essence has been buried deeply within. It is part of oneself that connects to God and that knows one's true purpose on earth. Generally, *neshamah* does not make itself known until well into adulthood.

Much of the life cycle is a long incubation period of self study, examination of goals and purpose, hopes and dreams. Inside, pressure builds when something hidden within begins to burst its outer shell. Suddenly, amid violent contractions an essential transition occurs. Something is born and something dies. Painfully or ecstatically, new levels of being are touched. This metaphor of metamorphosis, the birth of the soul is what Jung called "the process of individuation."

When the soul has been born, we suddenly know more, understand more and sense the inner meaning of things. We become ourselves a source of deeper wisdom. Although it may not be expressed in conventional ways, we become more religious. Left-brain logic and right-brain emotion and intuition become more evenly balanced.

This archetypal experience resonates in all human beings. Each culture expresses it in its own mythology. It forms the core of pre-Christian Greek and Roman mystery religion, pre-Israelite Middle Eastern religions, Christianity's dying and resurrecting god-man, medieval alchemy's "changing base metals into gold." Torah expresses this process through *aggadah* or *midrash*, its mythic saga of the soul's journey.

Experience 9

Guidance from Torah

Find out which weekly section of the Torah or *sidrah* is on the calendar for the coming Shabbat. You can find this on a Jewish calendar or by calling a local synagogue.

As you prepare to read the *sidrah*, spend five minutes in silence, keeping your mind still. Spend several more minutes focusing your full awareness on the fact that this Torah reading has something essential to tell you.

Formulate a question for which you'd like the Torah's guidance.

Read the *sidrah* with your mind open to whatever Torah has to teach you. Feel free to engage in the *midrash* process when it feels appropriate.

❖

Chapter 4

Halakhah – The Way

The Hebrew word for Jewish Law is *halakhah*, which comes from the root HaLaKh meaning "to walk" or "to go." The best translation is "the way." The image of "the Way" or "the Path" recurs throughout the world's religions. *Tao*, a major component of Chinese religion, literally means "The Way". Christianity was originally called "prohodos", the Way, and Jesus called himself, "The Way, the truth and the life" (JOHN 14:6).

Reaching the goal of spiritual experience requires discipline. Most of us must go through a long period of instruction and practice, or undergo intense instruction for a limited time at a specially designated place, such as *yeshivah* or *ashram* or *zendo*.

In every path, there are particular practices which help facilitate spiritual experience. In the *Bhagavad Gita*, Krishna counsels Arjuna to practice *karmayoga*, the Way of Selfless Action. American Indian shamans direct their people to avoid certain food or places at certain times. One of Islam's five central pillars is the observance of *Ramadan*, a thirty-day dawn to dusk fast.

In most traditions, meditation, prayer, fasting and dietary regulations, study, breath control, sexual restrictions, dance, singing, celebration, sacrifice, direction of attitude and contemplation are the common components of spiritual discipline.

Almost any human activity, however, can become a doorway

to spiritual experience. In a brief and beautiful book, *Zen In The Art of Archery*[1], Eugen Harrigel relates how he was a German professor of philosophy who studied archery in Japan with the Master Kenzo Awa. Following long years of study of the proper actions and meanings associated with the simple gesture of pulling a bow and releasing the arrow, Herrigel arrived at a state of transformation. He surrendered his sense of individuality and became a selfless vehicle through which the perfection of his art flowed.

Halakhah is the Jewish manifestation of intense spiritual discipline. It is the application of the one-pointed-ness of consciousness which ultimately causes transformation. To create change requires technology. Halakhah is a sacred technology that makes spiritual development possible.

Halakhah consists of small component activities which add up to something greater than themselves. Every aspect of human life relates to some aspect of *halakhah*, from birth to death, from waking each morning to retiring each night. Performing the components of life with the proper frame of mind elevates the activity from a simple survival need or recreational pursuit, into an action in the service of God.

In this way, *halakhah* unites the physical with the spiritual in every human activity. *Halakhah* is firmly rooted in the world, but at the same time it reveals the spiritual dimension of mundane events. For example, one small aspect of *halakhah* stipulates that the fiber content in clothes must not mix linen and wool (LEVITICUS 19:19, DEUTERONOMY 22:11), and thus reminds us of the Divine presence even in the activity of making cloth and choosing garments. Conversely, *halakhah's* specified ritual to celebrate the awesomeness of the birthday of the creation of the world is to play a simple tune on a ram's horn (*shofar*).

Halakhah focuses upon some of the most mundane human activities. The archetypal Jewish holy person is not a wandering

---

[1] Vintage Books, New York, 1953, 1971.

ascetic who has renounced the world, but a married householder who is active in all aspects of community life and pays the bills on time. *Halakhah* tends to be behavioristic rather that humanistic. It begins with doing an activity even if it does not seem instantly attractive or rewarding. Doing the activity facilitates the understanding of the activity. It is as if *halakhah* counsels, "Enough talk, just do it!"

Halakhah makes no distinction between ethical/moral actions and spiritual/religious actions. It demands moral behavior at all times and equates ethical behavior with the highest form of Divine service. Banal matters such as the payment of wages and fiscal policies are important aspects of *halakhah*. Honesty, fairness, respect and justice are preeminent Jewish virtues and manifesting them brings one closer to the experience of God.

Halakhah intertwines with all three aspects of the Soul, the *nefesh*, the *ru'ah* and the *neshamah*. A single act performed according to *halakhah's* directions involves and benefits all three.

Contrary to the misconception that *halakhah* is overly concerned with justice and law, most aspects of *halakhah* reflect great love and compassion for all living things. *Halakhah* balances both law and love. The highest form of Jewish spiritual development is manifest in the person who acts both fairly and compassionately, even if to the detriment of personal advantage. If *halakhah* seems to lack compassion, it may be because it regulates individuals more than they would like to be regulated.

Kavannah and *Mizvot*

Halakhah is concerned with the action itself far more that the intention or rationale, or the outcome. *Kavannah* is the Hebrew word for the intention and intensity behind an action. The ideal is right actions (*halakhah*) with proper intention (*kavannah*). The next step down is right action without *kavannah*, which is generally preferable to wrong action, or no action, with *kavannah*. The lowest rung of the ladder is wrong or no action with no spiritual intention.

Halakhah is derived from the Torah's 613 specific *miẓvot* —
translated literally as "commandments." A more accurate translation is "spiritual actions." Of the 613 instructions God pronounced to the Israelites, 365 are negative, "You shall nots" —
corresponding to the days of the year; 248 are positive, corresponding to the bones of the body. Performance of *miẓvot*,
or acting in accordance with *halakhah* is Judaism's "Way" to closeness to God.

Jews often perceive *halakhah* as an overinflated parent, a relentless superego, inflicting counterproductive guilt and resentment.
Often, Jews learn about its demands without gleaning the spiritual process *halakhah* facilitates. Most contemporary Jews act consciously in accordance with The Way only a small part of the time.
Many of us perform some *miẓvot*, but without the awareness of
the many levels of their significance.

On the flip side, Jews whose lives are guided by *halakhah* are
often overburdened by its demands. They tend to be stiff, controlled, even neurotically concerned with details.

In either case, *halakhah* is not an easy path. It requires careful navigation between the Scylla of unspiritual indifference and
the Charybdis of equally unspiritual compulsions. Unfortunately,
many Jews who grow up on one side or the other find themselves hopelessly estranged from Judaism as a whole.

Dietary Regulations — *Kosher* Vegetarianism

When God created the first human creatures of the Earth, God
blessed them with the words, "I give you every seed-bearing plant
that is upon the earth, and every tree that has seed bearing fruit.
They shall be yours for food" (GENESIS 1:29). No mention is made
of Earthlings eating other animals until after the world has been
destroyed in the Primordial Flood. God says to Noah, "Every
creature that lives shall be yours to eat. You must not, however,
eat flesh with its life blood in it" (GENESIS 8: 3-4). God had in-

tended that we be vegetarians, but it was impossible. The world had grown corrupt; God became more realistic. Eating meat was now permitted to all human beings, but with a restriction: It must be dead and cooked. This is a definition of being "minimally civilized," and it requires "knowledge of fire," the literal translation of "technology." Enlightenment at Sinai calls for much stricter dietary regulations than being "minimally civilized."

Most of us today buy food antiseptically pre-wrapped in plastic and styrofoam. It is easy to forget the significance of food in overall human development, and in our own individual growth. In earlier days, the process of growing, preparing and eating food consumed a large percent of life energy. Even today, the earliest memories most people can recall deal with food. The earliest known religious experiences were sacrifices, meals shared with gods.

We are what we eat. The meaning of the adage is that what we eat describes our culture. Furthermore, because the chemical components of the food we are the building blocks of our body, the food we eat determines who we are physically and emotionally as well.

Most tribes and cultures have particular animals, or parts of animals, which it deems wrong to consume. We often think of the "sacred cows" of India, blithely roaming the streets among starving people.

According to the *halakhah*, food is essential to facilitating the Jewish experience of God. A great deal of the Torah prescribes sacrifices which were practiced for hundreds of years. Another large part of the Torah describes which food is fit for consumption, and which is not. The original intention of *halakhah* was to limit meat-eating almost to the point of vegetarianism.

Kashrut — The Laws of Kosherness

Kosher means "fit," as in fit for consumption. *Kashrut* means "the laws of kosherness." *Kashrut*, which derives from a number of the Torah's *mizvot*, is a series of regulations that increases our awareness of the food we eat. *Kashrut* permits eating meat under deliberately difficult conditions. While less stringent than total vegetarianism, vegetarianism is certainly less complicated.

Kashrut does not regulate what grows from the ground. All fruits and vegetables are kosher. The general principle of *Kashrut* is that only healthy living animals from approved species, which have been killed and prepared properly are fit to consume:

— Animals must have cloven hooves and chew a cud (LEVITICUS 11:3). Therefore, pigs, rabbits, dogs, cats, snakes and elephants are forbidden. Cattle, sheep, goats, deer, bison and giraffes meet the criteria.

— The Torah lists certain birds which are excluded, mostly birds of prey: vultures, eagles, falcons, hawks, owls, pelicans and storks. Chicken, turkey, ducks and geese are permitted.

— Fish and sea creatures must have fins and scales (LEVITICUS 11:10). Whales, dolphins, lobster, shrimp, clams and crabs are forbidden. Most fish is permitted.

— Animals and birds (but not fish) must be slaughtered in a particular humane manner which involves slitting the wind-pipe, esophagus and jugular, resulting in instant death.

— All traces of blood must be removed from the meat. No rare, or even medium-rare steaks.

— Milk and milk products cannot be mixed with meat and meat products, including birds but not fish. No cheeseburgers or veal Parmesan. Separate dishes and cooking utensils for meat products are required.

— The hindquarters of animals are not permitted, unless special procedures are employed. This means no prime rib.

Eating animals implies a number of uncomfortable realities. Most significantly, it involves murder. The process of killing animals is bloody and distasteful. The act of killing a creature, or even eating it, diminishes one's compassion for living beings. Finally, an animal about to be killed is filled with fear and anger. Those emotions accompany chemical and hormonal changes which might affect whoever consumes it. *Kashrut* is Judaism's way of making us face these realities. It makes us aware at each meal that all life has been created by God and that God's presence is manifest with us.

Kashrut and the Eating of Meat

Kashrut doesn't want eating meat to become an easy thing to do. Pigs and rabbits, the easiest and cheapest meat sources yet developed, are forbidden. *Kashrut* includes a series of regulations pertaining to the raising and maintenance of livestock. Any animal eaten must be healthy, as animals can pass along their diseases. A post-mortem examination must be performed to verify the animal's health. Since all animals are what they eat as well, the animals themselves must be raised on kosher food. Shellfish are forbidden because they eat dead sealife; birds of prey because they eat both animals and carrion.

When an animal is slaughtered the procedure is a religious ritual. Eating meat becomes less offensive because its slaughter and preparation have been elevated to a spiritual act. The slaughterer (*shohet*) is a respected religious functionary who must have a commitment to a spiritual life. He recites a special blessing before taking an animal's life. The blade of his knife is perfectly sharp in order to spare the animal unnecessary pain.

The animal's blood, in which *nefesh* resides (LEVITICUS 17:11), must be quickly drained. Either broiling the meat or curing it in salt further removes the blood. Until then, the animal is "not quite dead."

Mixing of Milk and Meat and the Legacy of Jacob's Wound

Meat products and milk products must be cooked in and eaten off of separate sets of utensils. The mixing of milk and meat, a common pagan practice, was forbidden in the Torah three times (EXODUS 23:19; 34:16; DEUTERONOMY 14:21). Many other cultures, such as China and India are disinclined to mix the two.

Milk and meat symbolize the two opposite extremes of *yin* and *yang*. Meat implies the activity of a living animal, overcome by the slaughterer's active power over life. Milk implies the nurturing, living-giving, receptive, feminine power which preserves life.

The separation of milk and meat is a prime example of Torah's overall tendency to keep different qualities separate. Different plants cannot be planted together, fibers cannot be woven together, different activities are restricted to certain times.

When Jacob wrestled with his mysterious adversary (GENESIS 32:26) he was left with a permanent limp. As a result, *halakhah* demands that the sciatic nerve must be removed before the animal's hindquarters are edible. This rule limits meat consumption further, and it is also a reminder that spiritual work can deeply wound both body and soul.

A common misconception maintains that *kashrut* is primarily concerned with physical health and that because of modern refrigeration and health laws, it has outlived its usefulness. In fact, the current most common rendition of *kashrut* is anything but healthy. Salting meat adds vast quantities of sodium; hoof-and-mouth disease is common in cattle and is infectious even in well cooked meat while trichinosis in pork is killed by cooking; many adaptations of *kashrut* include high cholesterol additions of animal fat.

The original purpose of *kashrut* was to limit intake of meat at a time when all meat was a luxury. Ironically, conveniently packaged kosher food is readily available throughout the West, complete with preservatives and other unhealthy chemical additives. *Kashrut's* intention is better served by eliminating or severely reducing meat, and by eliminating kosher packaged products which are overloaded with chemicals and additives.

Experience 10

Experiencing *Kashrut*

Take an inventory of your own diet for several days. Notice your accidental — or intentional — observance of *kashrut*. For each of the following categories of food, ask yourself if you eat them at home or outside home:
— pork products
— shellfish
— non-kosher beef, lamb, chicken, etc.
— cheeseburgers
— prepackaged foods containing animal fat
— food prepared and/or served on un-kosher utensils and dishes (that is, used for both meat and milk products).
— any type of meat or meat product

Choose one of these categories that you currently consume and resolve not to eat anything from it for the next two weeks. Whenever an opportunity arises to eat that food, remind yourself that by avoiding it you are accepting an opportunity for spiritual growth.

If you slip and forget, or if the lobster looks too delicious, do not judge yourself a failure. Remind yourself that you can do differently the next time if you so choose.

❖

Shabbat: Spiritual Time

Shabbat is the seventh day. "On the seventh day, God finished all the work he had been doing...and designated it *kodesh*, holy" (GENESIS 2:23).

The essence of *Shabbat* is to be *kodesh*. *Kodesh*, or holy, means "different," "unusual," "set apart for a special, higher purpose." Torah attributes *kedushah* (holiness) to a variety of activities and institutions. *Kedushah* is particularly distinctive of *Shabbat*. *Shabbat*, a regular period of time set aside for spiritual work, recognizes that technology, for all its attributes, is an obstacle to spiritual development. *Shabbat* is based on the premise that alternate states of consciousness are experienced through a rejection of technology and an embrace of a higher vision.

Shabbat is a celebration of right-brain activity, the half which predominates in imaginary, receptive, spontaneous, emotional, intuitive activity. *Halakhah* governing *Shabbat* forbids left-brain activity, the side which governs dominating technology. For twenty-five hours the order of things is simply allowed to "be." A day of total right-brain activity is not easy to achieve. It means avoiding electricity, telephones, television, travel except by foot, working, writing, building, creating or destroying. Plants are not to be picked, medicines are not to be taken (unless urgently needed). With this respite from left-brain activity, the right brain can exercise. *Shabbat* is a temporary rejection of the modern world, a retreat into the mysteries of non-linear timelessness and "placelessness" of the right brain.

Each *Shabbat* recalls the first *Shabbat*, the creation of the world. On this day we step outside of time and see the creation as if it were brand new. At the same time, *Shabbat* is a foretaste of "the World to Come" (*olam ha-ba*), loosely translated as "eternity." The exact nature of *olam haba*, an afterlife or future life, is rarely defined, but *Shabbat* alludes to it. Thus, each *Shabbat* includes every *Shabbat* from the beginning of time to time's conclusion.

On *Shabbat* we are not the same people as we are the other days of the week. The *neshamah*, the Higher Self, is able to connect with God more easily. In addition, it is supplemented with *neshamah yeterah*, an "additional *neshamah*." The experience of operating out of the right brain gives the impression that "something extra has been added." We are using what usually lies dormant. On one level, the notion of an "additional soul" is a perfect poetic image to describe the different experience. It is also a profound metaphysical insight. If we are changed in that moment, we acquire a new reality which is available to carry back into the other six days of the week.

The Many Aspects of God and *Shabbat*

God has many names, each name indicating a different aspect of how God is experienced. There are two primary aspects: immanently, as when God seems to be "within," and transcendently, when God is "out there." When we experience either one or the other, we're grasping one aspect of an undifferentiated whole. One of God's names is *Shekhinah*, which means "proximity." *Shekhinah* refers to God's receptive/feminine/right-brain/*yin* aspects. *Shekhinah* also implies immanence, the God within.

Shabbat is a time when *Shekhinah* is even closer and more accessible. Another name for *Shabbat* is *kallah*, the archetypal bride. *Shabbat* is welcomed as a bride is welcomed to the marriage canopy. The Friday evening meal that begins *Shabbat* is a bridal banquet.

The corresponding transcendent, male name of God is *Hakadosh Barukh Hu*, "The Holy Blessed One." On *Shabbat*, the *Shekhinah* and *Hakadosh Barukh Hu* are locked into an embracing, loving union. But the intimacy is not to be taken lightly. *Shabbat* is also called *malkah*, the queen, and this day is afforded the highest honors and respect. Anything as right-brain oriented as *Shabbat* risks the danger of falling into triviality, personal whims and ephemerality. The image of the queen gives the *Shabbat* experience stability and permanence.

A Typical Shabbat

Shabbat is a programmed sequence of diverse moods, activities and experiences. *Shabbat* begins with an "at home" celebration, initiated by lighting candles, joyfully drinking a bit of wine, and savoring the earthiness of bread sprinkled with a pinch of salt. The family grouping eats, sings and dances. *Shabbat* eve is a nostalgic look backward at the old ways. The evening's mood is one of harmony and abundance, relief and expansion. Late Friday night is a particularly propitious time for lovemaking.

Shabbat morning is quiet, reflective and intellectual. It is celebrated at Synagogue with the community. With a variety of songs, dances, prayers, and teachings, the *Shabbat* morning service facilitates a particular set of spiritual experiences. Study of Torah predominates the service, and the removal of the Torah from its place in the ark is the dramatic high point.

Shabbat afternoon is a time of yearning, longing and dreaming for what is yet to come. It is a time for imagining and visualizing potential, and also a time to reflect on what corrections need to be made when the proper time comes. The melodies of the afternoon are slow and lingering, the food simple and every taste savored.

As *Shabbat* concludes, the mood becomes hopeful, relaxed and satisfied. It's a time to be with friends, tell stories, and resolve which actions will be part of the spiritual growth program for the upcoming week. At *Shabbat's* departure, all time stops for a brief ceremony called *havdalah*, "separation," which includes candlelight, wine and spices. The candlelight includes a hypnotic, consciousness-altering flicker. The sip of wine, which began *Shabbat*, now concludes it. The ultimateness of the moment is augmented with spices, usually myrtle, clove and cinnamon. Elijah, the prophet who never died and whose return will initiate the messianic climax of history, is invited to be present for just one moment, during which the end of all time is made present and the world is perfect. *Shabbat* concludes with the blessing *shavuah tov*, "A good week."

Experience 11

Experiencing *Shabbat*

Although the act you will perform to begin *Shabbat*, lighting two candles and reciting a short blessing over them, will take only a few minutes, your preparation and its after effects will last considerably longer. Although the candle lighting is usually a women's task, men may perform it as well.

Call the weather bureau and find out the exact time of sunset.

Select a pair of special candlesticks. Pay attention to their beauty, history and origin, their personal significance to you. If you don't have candlesticks, acquire a pair with care and consideration.

Acquire candles with the same care. Choose some that are attractive or give off a pleasant fragrance.

On Friday evening plan to have your house cleaned and your dinner prepared by at least an hour before sunset. Warn those you live with that you will need time to yourself at sunset, or invite them to join you.

About fifty minutes before sunset, put the candles in the candlesticks and place them in an honored spot in your home.

Spend ten minutes in silent meditation about the act you are about to perform: When you light these candles you will become God's partner. This is a special, sacred task. When you light these candles you will be broadcasting light, and bringing light into darkness. You will be performing a dance as your emotions move through you. You will be beginning *Shabbat*. Be aware of the gears shifting within you.

No later than eighteen minutes before the moment of sundown, cover your head to remind you that God is above you, close your eyes to remind you that God is within you, and light the candles.

Recite the traditional blessing and feel free to be expressive.

Barukh ata Adonai	We praise you, Adonai
Eloheinu, melekh ha-olam	Our God who rules all the universe
Asher kiddshanu	Who sanctifies us
B'mizvotav	with commandments
Ve-zivanu	And commands us
Le-hadlik ner shel Shabbat	to light Shabbat candles

Spend ten minutes after lighting the candles luxuriating in the intensity of the mood. Stay in this space until you're ready to leave.

Continue with the *kiddush* over wine and *mozi* over bread (You can find these in any Jewish prayerbook. If you don't have one, obtain one as part of your *Shabbat* preparations.). Say them in English rather than Hebrew if you prefer.

Enjoy a leisurely, relaxing dinner. Let nothing disturb your mood of relaxation. Make an effort to keep the conversation on a higher level than usual. Sing a song or two.

Stay home for the evening. Do not turn any appliances (especially tv) on or off. Read the Torah *sidrah* and reflect on what it says to you. If it's appropriate to your relationship, open yourself to the possibility of love making.

Saturday morning attend synagogue. Arrive early, stay late. Let yourself experience the ritual deeply and fully. Notice your moods, but without judgment.

After service, stay for the *kiddush*, the social hour.

Ask yourself if you wish to continue this *Shabbat* experience. If not, praise yourself for your accomplishment and go on to other things. If you choose to continue, spend the rest of the afternoon taking a walk, napping, visiting with friends and family, meditating, observing nature.

Saturday evening ends *Shabbat* forty-two minutes after sundown with the brief, beautiful ritual of *havdalah*, or separation. You will need a special braided candle with more than one wick, a jar of sweet spices (such as clove and cinnamon) and a glass of wine, filled to the brim. You will again need your prayerbook. Light the candle and meditate on its flame. Say the appropriate blessings. Invite Elijah to join you for a moment. Then extinguish the candle by dipping it in the wine. *Shabbat* is over. Wish everyone *shavuah tov*, "a good week."

Ask yourself what you have learned from this experience; Are you likely to do it again?

❖

Festivals: Emotional Calisthenics

Jewish festivals occur each year on the same date of the Jewish calendar, which is different from our Western Gregorian calendar. The Jewish calendar is similar to the ancient Babylonian calender. Each month begins with the appearance of the new moon. With 12 lunar months of 29½ days or only 354 days in a year, seven times every nineteen years there is a leap year in which a whole month is added.

To calculate the Jewish year, add 3760 to the Gregorian year (between Rosh HaShana and December 31 add 3761). The creation of the world according to the genealogies of the Torah and subsequent history puts the date of creation at about 6000 years ago. Obviously, few modern Jews believe the world is only that many years old, but rather the genealogies are subject to serious *aggadah*-ization: The first six "days" of creation were much longer than twenty-four hours each.

The Jewish festivals commemorate historic events, while at the same time they note the changes in the seasons. Festivals have deep psychological and spiritual meanings, and for each one *halakhah* prescribes a mood and set of accompanying behaviors. In order to experience these moods, *halakhah* provides the needed training. As a result of this training, ones experience of life becomes richer and more intense.

The annual holiday cycle is a workable program to re-invigorate our ability to feel. Our ability to feel is partly spontaneous, partly conditioned, depending upon whether our parents encouraged or discouraged childhood tears, fears, and tantrums, reinforced or knocked down our self-esteem, pride or humility. That ability to feel becomes remolded and either blunted or sharpened through our growing up process. Each holiday has a mood, and the *halakhah* for that holiday helps us feel that mood more deeply at regular intervals throughout the lifecycle.

Holidays also provide a steamvalve to let off a bit of our pent-up selves. For a short time every year, we are permitted, even encouraged, to express an untapped part of our emotional makeup.

Purim

Purim is the happiest, silliest and most carefree day of the Jewish year. It comes in late February or early March when winter is barely over and everyone is ready to celebrate. Children dress up in costumes and adults throw caution to the wind in celebration of the rescue of the Jews of Persia about 2500 years ago. As described in the Book of Ester, *Purim* is the one day of the year when getting drunk is encouraged, and satirizing Torah and community leaders is most appropriate.

When we celebrate *Purim* we learn to be uninhibited. Even those individuals with a tendency toward being depressed have a chance to experience elation.

Tishah Be-Av

The saddest day of the Jewish year is the ninth day of the month of Av (*Tishah Be-Av*). It falls during the "dog days" of late July to early August. It is a day of national mourning for the two destructions of Jerusalem in 586 BCE and 70 CE. Many practices associated with mourning a loved one are part of its *halakhah*: fasting, sitting on the floor, wearing no leather, singing dirges.

When we celebrate this holiday, we learn to cry and mourn. It is something we need to learn, for the death of loved ones is inevitable. The emotions that emerge at this time of transition are so intense and foreign to us that we often don't know what to feel or how to behave. *Tishah Be-Av* gives us an opportunity to practice.

Purim and *Tishah Be-Av* are the two extremes, with the moods of the other holidays falling somewhere in between. Granted, not many people these days get drunk on *Purim* or shed tears on *Tishah Be-Av*. The *halakhah* for the festivals has been bleached into homogenized consistency by our technological age. Some of the other festivals fare better, but even the best are a mere shadow of what they once were or could be.

Rosh HaShana and the High Holy Days

The High Holy Day season (late September-early October) is the most intense period for spiritual work in the Jewish year. It begins with *Rosh HaShana*, the New Year, the Birthday of the World. Its dominant mood is jubilation, and a hopeful sense of putting away the old to start anew. At the same time, it is intensely prayerful and hopeful. The ram's horn, or *shofar*, is a special symbol of this festival. Its plaintive wail is a hotline between the human heart and God.

The week between *Rosh HaShana* and *Yom Kippur* is a mild, low-key period of introspection and supplication for mercy. It carries awareness that the Day of Judgment is coming, and God may not be pleased.

Yom Kippur

This is the most serious day of the Jewish year, a rehearsal for our own death. *Halakhah* prescribes that we dress in shrouds, refrain from all physical pleasures and look at ourselves most deeply and critically. It is a day of total fasting, abstinence and prayer. It is a time to see our shortcomings and humbly beg forgiveness. This rehearsal of death makes us aware of our own finitude, and of the fact that one day we will return to God. When the final *shofar* sounds, we are recalled to life, renewed and spiritually expanded.

Sukkot

Along with the High Holy Days, the most important holidays are the three pilgrimage festivals, *Sukkot*, *Pesah* and *Shavuot*, so called because in ancient times their rituals included pilgrimage to Jerusalem. *Sukkot* comes right after the High Holy Days, and serves as an antidote to *Yom Kippur's* heaviness. *Sukkot*, which means "tents," is a one week outdoor camping trip, a joyful thanksgiving, a harvest festival. It also recalls the Israelites' experience as desert nomads between slavery and the Promised Land. To celebrate *Sukkot*, *halakhah* dictates that participants move out of their homes and live in a tent for a week to learn what it meant to be human before nature was controlled. This holiday is a community building event, as people must rely on each other during this week of living close to the earth. At present, technology has so estranged us from nature and Mother Earth has been so abused, that *Sukkot's* message is particularly poignant.

Sukkot concludes with *Shmini Atzeret*, "The Eighth Assembly." This day counterbalances the joyful community of the preceding week. It is a moment to reflect on the fact that we are at the mercy of God and that without the support of nature, we would not survive.

Simkḥat Torah

The day after *Sukkot* is *Simkḥat Torah*, "The Rejoicing of the Torah." The weekly *sidrah* cycle of Torah readings begins and ends on this day. *Halakhah* prescribes ecstatic singing and dancing and parading around with the Torah. Next to *Purim*, it's the most joyous day of the year, though it lacks *Purim's* burlesque character. Like *Purim*, it's considered a children's holiday. Unfortunately, adults forget they have a "child within" who needs such a celebration.

Pesaḥ

Of the three pilgrimage festivals, *Pesaḥ*, or Passover, has retained most of its vigor. It comes in early spring, when rebirth is the most obvious human emotion. Passover not only celebrates the "Letting Go of Egypt," but recreates the experience.

Like a psychodrama, *Pesaḥ* is celebrated in the home with a special meal called the *seder*. This meal is a celebration of the Exodus during which each participant feels as if he or she were personally going out of Egypt. *Halakhah* determines special food, songs, stories and prayers and a special textbook of programmed pedagogy to recreate the experience of liberation.

Omer

Omer is a seven week period which falls between *Pesaḥ* and *Shavuot*, and is characterized by a certain apprehension about the health of the spring crops. Celebrations are avoided during this time, and *halakhah* does not allow weddings to take place. From *Omer* we learn patience, that growth comes slowly, ripening in its own time.

Shavuot

Shavuot ("Weeks") is the Festival of Enlightenment. Seven weeks, hence the name, after the Exodus, the Israelites received enlightenment at Sinai. *Shavuot*, celebrated in May to early June, seven weeks after *Pesaḥ*, is also the festival of the ripening of the first fruits. When our ancestors received the Torah at Sinai, they stayed up all night studying it. On the eve of *Shavuot*, we commemorate that moment by doing the same. There is something remarkable about "pulling an all-nighter." It makes us reach into regions of the psyche seldom touched. When the night is spent with a small group of colleagues engaged in Torah, the effect is overwhelming.

Ḥanuka

This minor holiday seems like a major one because it falls on the lunar equivalent of winter solstice. This is the time of year which most demands a holiday. The short days and cold weather create a general depression which is assuaged by gathering with loved ones, lighting candles, singing songs and eating potato *latkes* (pancakes). Commemorating a military victory which established Jewish independence 2200 years ago, *Ḥanuka* spiritualizes the hard political realities of the struggle for freedom in the face of oppression and coercion.

New Moon

The appearance of every new moon is a minor Jewish holiday. It hints at a time when matriarchy was the common form of social and spiritual organization. Throughout the world's history, the moon's monthly cycle of waxing and waning and the mysterious feeling it engenders has made the moon the primary symbol of the feminine/*yin* aspect of nature. Until patriarchy took over, the moon was identified with the greatest goddess. At the present time, with the empowerment of women growing on a global level, the new moon ceremony is beginning to regain its archetypal power.

The Holocaust And The Birth Of Modern Israel

There are two recent additions to the otherwise ancient Hebrew calendar which mark events in our own time, the Holocaust and the birth of the modern State of Israel. The external events of this world and the internal evolution of the soul are two sides of the same coin. Jewish spiritual growth is always firmly ground- ed in Jewish history, both ancient and modern. *Yom Hasho'ah*, Holocaust Day, is as incomprehensible as the event. The joy of *Yom Ha'azma'ut* (Independence Day) is restrained by the polit- ical realities surrounding present day Israel. The juxtaposition of these two days within a week (in late spring) parallels that of the destruction of European Jewry and the modern rebirth of a Jewish state in the Land of Israel within a decade. The modern tendency to assume that events of mythological significance only happened centuries ago is challenged by these observances.

Experience 12

Celebrating a Holiday

Check a Jewish calendar or local synagogue and find out when the next holiday takes place.

Investigate some of the details of the *halakhah* for the holiday.

Choose several aspects of the observance which appeal to you, and prepare to do them.

When the holiday arrives, do the observances and also spend the day concentrating on the day's special mood. Try to feel whatever it is you're supposed to feel the entire day.

When the holiday is over, ask yourself:

Did I really feel it?
How intense did the feeling become?
Did I resist intensifying the feeling?
Did the feeling begin to transcend its emotional base into a
    deeper spiritual experience?
What did I learn?

❖

Davening: Sacrificial Prayers or Prayer Sacrifices

Until the Temple of Jerusalem was destroyed by the Romans
in 70 CE, the sacrifices were the Jewish central spiritual activity.
While the Temple stood, prayer, meditation, song, dance and
most other spiritual activity was of secondary importance.
However, when the Temple was destroyed, virtually all sacrifice
was suspended. As Jewish theology has continued to unfold, the
belief has been that one day, when the Messiah arrives, the Temple will be rebuilt and the sacrifices reinstated.

Korban, Hebrew for sacrifice, derives from the root meaning
"to draw near." A sacrifice is an offering of food which "draws
us near" to God. Obviously, God doesn't need our food, but
the act of setting it aside for God is a powerful human experience.
It allows us to open to God's presence when God eats with us.
Many of the sacrifices of the Temple were offerings of grain or
fruit. Sometimes animals were slaughtered and cooked.

At first glance, sacrifice may seem like something outside of
modern experience. However, in Christian tradition, the sacrificial meal has remained a preeminent element in the spiritual
path. The Eucharist, or Communion, is a meal that is eaten in
which God becomes part of those who eat it.

Experience 13

Imagining a Sacrifice

Read Leviticus, Chapter 4 in the Torah.
Read it again, this time more slowly, picturing the whole scene
as though it were a documentary film. You may want to write
or dictate your images.
Ask yourself:
How do I feel about sacrifices?
Does the experience of seeing animals slaughtered and
barbecued on an altar affect me very much?
Am I repulsed or inspired?
Does it make me feel close to God, or does it make me sick?

❖

We have only a few remnants of sacrifices today, one of which
is called *kaporet*. Practiced by only a small subset of very traditional Jews, it refers to the slaughter of a chicken on the day before *Yom Kippur* in the hope that the act will remove whatever
impedes the offerer from drawing closer to God on this most
significant day. In addition, when we bake *hallah*, a special bread
for *Shabbat* eve, we separate a pinch of dough as a reminder
of the original *hallah*, the bread sacrifice that was part of the
Temple ritual.
More often however, we read about the sacrifices as a substitute for doing them. Each morning's worship service includes
a description of ancient, daily sacrifices. Several *sidrah's* of the
Torah consist totally of these descriptions. To our modern ears,
sacrifices don't sound like something that will facilitate spirituality, but sacrifices scratch at something deep within our psyche.
Essentially, human beings haven't changed very much in the

last few thousand years. We still have the same emotions and
needs, though they are defined and met differently. Killing
animals and splashing their blood about on an altar revolts most
of us, while it inspired our ancestors. Something which now lies
buried within us was manifest closer to the surface of our fore-
bears. The "savage within" has been well described in modern
psychology. Freud called it the *id*, and Jung understood it as the
archetype of the shadow. Reading about sacrifices provides us
with a connection to our primitive past. Instead of making
sacrifices, we "draw near" through davening.

Davening is translated as "prayer," but is really a hybrid word:
a Yiddish root related to the English word "devotion," and to
the Sanskrit *deva*, "a Divine Figure," with an English participial
suffix to describe an activity performed in Hebrew. In ancient
times, sacrifices were mandated three times a day, with extra
sacrifices on *Shabbat*, new moons and festivals. Today, there is
a round of davening designated for each ancient sacrifice.

Along with *kashrut*, *Shabbat* and festivals, davening is one
of the most essential aspects of the Way. Davening is the central
activity of synagogue services, and is the primary process for drawing close to God. The role of meditation in Buddhist and Hindu traditions, dance in the Sufi-Islamic tradition, and the
Eucharist in the Christian tradition belongs to davening in Jewish tradition. If you want to experience God in the traditional,
time honored Jewish way, you must learn to *daven*.

Unfortunately, it is not the easiest skill to master. The first
hurdle is that davening requires a minimal working knowledge
of Hebrew. It is possible to *daven* in English, though it loses
much of its poetic power. In addition, davening involves a dance,
special accoutrements, a knowledge of the service and openness
to the experience of prayer.

Davening's dance consists of gentle rhythmic swaying of the
whole body, called *shukkling*, throughout the service. Davening's accoutrement (traditionally worn only by men, though this
is currently changing) consists of a *tallit*, a prayer shawl with spe-

cial macramé tied at the corners, and leather amulets called *tefillin* containing verses from the Torah which are bound to the head and arm on weekday mornings. The familiar skull cap (*yarmulke* in Yiddish, *kippah* in Hebrew) is nothing more than a simple headcovering. It derives from an old custom that men cover their heads as a sign of respect, the exact opposite of contemporary Western practice.

All davening experiences share the same few basic elements:

— the introduction
— the *Shema* and her blessings
— the *Prayer*
— reading from the Torah
— the conclusion

The *Shabbat* morning service lasts about two and one half hours, and includes all these components. The weekday afternoon service includes only the *Prayer* and takes five minutes.

The introduction lasts about forty-five minutes on *Shabbat* morning, ten minutes on weekday mornings and is absent from afternoon and evening services. The introduction, which latecomers usually miss, can be the most spiritually evocative part of the entire service. It epitomizes davening's most characteristic pattern: everyone reads the same page or paragraph independently at the same time. The leader of the service reads the first line aloud, then each person reads through the paragraph or page softly, or silently, with whatever speed, intonation, inflection and punctuation that feels right. The leader then reads the last line aloud, indicating it's time to go on. Participating in this forty-five minute long, low-key, inwardly directed devotional exercise, draws the participant more deeply into him or herself and closer to God.

The introduction begins with a series of blessings that focus attention on body and soul, on Torah and *mizvot*, and on who we are and why we are created. It continues with selections from the Torah and Talmud dealing with the sacrifices whose reading reminds us of davening's precursor. It then goes on to a series of selections from the Torah and Book of Psalms which shift our attention to God and God's power manifest in nature and history.

Experience 14

Davening in Hebrew or English

Attend any morning synagogue service. (Call in advance to check times on service so you can arrive on time.)

Pay particular attention to the introductory section of the davening. Note the sing-song cadence that characterizes the leader's reading aloud of the first and last lines. Try to mimic the cadence, either in Hebrew or English, at first silently and then perhaps saying the words softly.

Note the general meaning of each paragraph and try to relate to it.

Note on types of Synagogues: Generally speaking, Reform Synagogues do not practice davening with the traditional cadences, but rather read the service straight. This "contemporization" of the ancient patterns made sense when it was adopted over a century ago, but its current legacy is an overly formalized procedure that ought to learn to dance. In doing this experience you will need either an Orthodox Synagogue, if the separation of male and female daveners is not too offensive to you, or a Conservative Synagogue, which combines davening with androgenous seating.

❖

The Shema and Her Blessings

The second section of the service is a meditation on the Oneness of God. *Shema* means "Listen!" and the *Shema* begins with, "Listen Israel! *YHYH* our God is the Infinite One *YHVH* of all time and space!" This section takes about twenty minutes to recite on *Shabbat*, and three minutes on weekdays. It is said silently, with all attention focused upon the depth of its message. The *Shema* is a series of three paragraphs from the Torah which remind us that 1) God is One and you must strive to make God's presence a reality every moment of your life (DEUTERONOMY 6: 4-9); 2) there are laws of causation or karma or *sekhar ve-onesh* that operate in the world and so you must respect the potential effects of all your deeds (DEUTERONOMY 11:13-21); and 3) you must strive to align your deeds to the demands of Torah, even those which seem trivial or strange (NUMBERS 15: 37-41).

The *Shema* is sandwiched between two blessings that precede it and one that follows. A blessing, or *berakhah*, begins with *Barukh ata Adonai*, "We praise you, *Adonai*," and then describes something for which we praise God. (*Adonai*, "My Lord," is the name of God most often verbally pronounced in davening.) The preceding blessings called respectively *Yotzer*, "Creation" and *Ahavah*, "Love," reaffirm that God has created the world and that God's love is manifest through Torah.

The blessing after the *Shema*, *Geulah*, "Redemption," reminds us that the proof of God's power and love was manifest in the release from Egypt, and by implication, our own release. Reflecting momentarily on each of the themes walks the *daven*-er through a set of paces which over time facilitates the experience of God's unity.

The *Prayer*

The third part of the service is "The *Prayer*," (*Tefillah*) or The Eighteen, called such because the weekday service originally had eighteen component benedictions. It now has nineteen on weekdays, seven on *Shabbat* and most festivals. The Eighteen is also called "Standing" (*Amida*) because it is said while standing. The *Prayer* is where we ask God for the strength and power to continue our appointed tasks.

If you were trying to persuade someone to do something, you would be wise to begin by establishing rapport, then making the pitch, and finally being thankful in advance for their help. This is the format of The *Prayer*.

The first three benedictions establish rapport. We address God by reminding God of our past relationship (this *brakhah* is called *Avot*, "Ancestors"), by acknowledging that God's power is all that creates life (this *berahkhah* is *Gevurot*, "Power"), and by joining together with all the spiritual beings of the universe and singing a chorale to the awe God evokes (the third, *kedushah*, "Holiness").

Now perhaps God will listen to our requests, which are only asked on weekdays. On *Shabbat* and festivals it is unseemly to bother God this way, so we substitute one benediction which praises God for the special moment now being experienced (*Kedushat HaYom*, "The Holiness of the Day"). On weekdays, we have a list of thirteen special requests, which are framed in the first person plural to temper the ego.

In the first three of our requests, we ask God for spiritual needs:

1) Give us wisdom (*Binah*, "wisdom").
2) Give us the strength to make changes (*Teshuvah*, "return").
3) Make us feel forgiveness and compassion (*Selikhah*, "forgiveness").

We next turn the focus of our requests to physical, emotional and material needs:

4) Give us strength in our suffering and our strivings (*Ge'ulah*, "redemption").

5) Heal our wounds and diseases (*Refu'ah*, "healing").
6) Give us prosperity all year (*Birkhat hashanim*, "the blessing of the year").

Our attention now turns to our community. We ask for:

7) The reunification of all Jews for their sacred purpose (*Kibbuz galuyot*, "regathering the exiles").
8) The rebalancing of justice and compassion on this earth (*Mishpat*, "justice").
9) The defeat of the forces of darkness that threaten us (*Haminim*, "the adversaries").
10) The support of those allied to light. (*Hazadikim*, "the Righteous").
11) The coming of the rebuilding of Jerusalem and the con-
& comitant coming of the Messiah who will bring about
12) the redemption of the Jewish people (*Yerushalayim*, "Jerusalem" and *David*, "The House of David").
13) That God will listen to all these requests (*Tefillah*, "prayer").

We end by thanking God for past, present and future help. With the three concluding benedictions, we remind God and ourselves that this prayer is in place of the sacrifice (*Rezei*, "Let it be"), that every moment of our lives depends on God's protection (*Hoda'ah*, "Acknowledgement"), and that what is most important is God's greatest gift, peace (*Shalom*, "peace").

Experience 15

Becoming More Familiar with the Service

Obtain a copy of the prayerbook, or *siddur*, if you don't already have one.

Find weekday morning service. Locate the *Shema* and her blessings and The *Prayer*.

Read each paragraph of those sections along with their explanations in this chapter.

Attach mental footnotes to any of the words you feel need additional clarification. Feel free to mentally rephrase or add words to any part of these sections that do not express what you feel.

Attend a weekday morning synagogue service and experience actually davening these sections. Say the words using the *Shema* and The *Prayer* as a vehicle for expressing your own feelings.

❖

Reading from the Torah

The fourth major element of the Jewish service is reading from the Torah, which is done on *Shabbat* and festival mornings in full form, and in abbreviated form on Monday and Thursday mornings and *Shabbat* afternoon. This reading is not simply reciting words, but reading from a spiritual text which speaks to our *neshamah*, Higher Self. It is a reading from the *sidrah*, so it is an oracle. We remove the Torah from its place in the Ark with pageantry that creates a psychodrama. For a moment, we are actually standing at Sinai, waiting to receive enlightenment.

On *Shabbat* and festival mornings, the reading from the Torah is supplemented by a selection from the Books of the Prophets (the *haftarah*). These Books follow the Torah and compose the second section of the Hebrew Bible. Their stories span the eight hundred years following the giving of the Torah. The selection from the Prophets develops one of the themes in the *sidrah* for the season of the year.

After the prophetic reading, the service usually includes a sermon by the rabbi, called a *d'var Torah*, a word of Torah, and it serves to intensify the weekly Torah lesson.

On *Shabbat* and festival mornings there is an additional reading of The *Prayer,* as there was an additional sacrifice at the Temple performed in honor of the day.

The final section consists of a few well known songs and two brief special prayers. One is the *Aleinu*, "It is our task," which sums up the davening experience by stating that our real task in this lifetime is *tikkum olam*, "mending the universe," working with God to complete the Creation of this world. The second concluding prayer is called *Kaddish*, a memorial prayer recited by those who have had a next of kin die in the previous year, or who observe the anniversary of the death of a next of kin. The recital of this prayer creates a connection between this physical plane and the etheric plane to which each *neshamah* is released at death.

Experience 16

Opening to Prayer

Choose something you want to pray for. Compose a short prayer asking God to grant your request. Pray this prayer at least three times a day for at least three days or longer.

Write down this prayer and tack it to your bulletin board or refrigerator where you'll see it often. On this same paper, write the names of the months in a list. After a week ask yourself if the answer to your prayer was "yes" or "no."

On the last day of the month, ask yourself the same question. Write the answer next to the month. On the last day of every month for the next year, ask yourself the question and record

the answer. Remember, a prayer is answered even if the answer
is "no" or "not now, maybe later."

❖

Personal Status: Who is a Jew and Who Can Marry One?

Halakhah takes rituals very seriously and stipulates essential
rituals for certain major life transitions. *Halakhah* doesn't acknowledge that two people have been married or divorced unless the proper rituals have been performed. Nor does it
acknowledge that someone has become a Jew unless the proper
ritual has been performed.

Halakhah also prescribes rituals for hundreds of minor actions and activities. One of the *miẓvot* about the *Pesaḥ* holiday
stipulates that any food that might have leavening agents in it
must be removed from the house. But, in the hard reality of
these economic times, none of us wants to throw out good food.
The answer is a ritual, in which we put all the half-consumed
packages of crackers, cookies and cereals in a special cupboard
and perform a ceremony in which we "sell them to someone else."
For the week of *Pesaḥ* they sit in the cupboard, but we don't
own the food or touch it and thus we have fulfilled the requirement of getting rid of it.

Doing a special ritual, even a formalistic, apparently silly ritual
like this one, creates a powerful inner experience. One danger
of *halakhah* is that we can become obsessive about the details
of ritual and block out the overall spiritual energy it facilitates.
Halakhah is demanding with many details which must be at-
tended to. All of them are tiles of a mosaic which facilitates the
experience of God. However, by dealing with its demands certain things become clearly defined. Once a ritual is properly done,

the status of a thing is absolute, with no grey areas left. As the *Pesaḥ* ritual shows, the spiritual requirements of *halakhah* can be stretched to accomodate material realities.

While various Jewish movements differ on how far *halakhah* can be stretched in terms of the spiritual and material import of the rituals, the one area where spiritual and material come closest together (and where Jews disagree most vehemently) is in the area of personal status. The most difficult questions *halakhah* generates are, "Who is a Jew?" and "Who can marry whom?"

According to the *halakhah*, there are two ways to become a Jew. One is through initiation. After sufficient study and spiritual growth, one goes through the proper rituals and becomes a Jew. These rituals consist of circumcision for males and immersion in a special ritual bath for everyone.

The other way to become a Jew is through birth. Being Jewish is transmitted on a physical level through the maternal line. If your mother is a Jew, so are you.

Because Jews differ about how far *halakhah* stretches, some Jews deny that some other Jews have the authority to properly supervise the rituals. In addition, some Jews now believe that it is time to allow transmission of being Jewish through the paternal line. These are major issues within the contemporary Jewish world.

Endogamy, marriage within the group, is another of those archetypal trends that the Jewish path has wholeheartedly maintained. Exogamy, marriage outside the group, has always been threatening to the maintenance of The Path. In most of the cultures Judaism has participated in, exogamy was strictly forbidden by the host nations. In these times it is no longer unusual though most Jews would still maintain that exogamy is the line beyond which *halakhah* cannot be stretched.

According to *halakhah*, divorce is possible, but unless the ritual is done properly the marriage is not dissolved.

Unfortunately, *halakhah* doesn't permit a woman to remarry without either a divorce or her husband's certified death. If a couple separates but the husband will not consent to divorce, or a husband wanders off and disappears, the wife becomes an *agunah*, a "bound woman" who is not allowed to remarry. *Halakhah* has found sufficient loopholes within itself to free men — but not women — from these categories. If she lives with someone without marriage and bears a child by such a union, the child is a *mamzer*, or "a tainted one." Such a child is considered a Jew, but he or she can only marry another *mamzer* or a convert to Judaism.

Halakhah is not a perfect system. The *agunah* and the *mamzer* represent the two extreme instances in which *halakhah's* ritual formality causes considerable discomfort. *Halakhah* has internal mechanisms for alleviating these situations. Unfortunately, some of *halakhah's* authorities have been unwilling to employ them.

There is a tendency among Jews and non-Jews to see aspects of *halakhah* as ridiculously demanding, especially within the context of modern American openess to alternative lifestyles. What it offers, at the very least, is an ideal, even if it borders on the extreme. Although some people are quite scrupulous about conducting every moment of their lives within *halakhah's* requirements, even most spiritually committed Jews are far from reaching all its demands.

However, when you are on the path, you are drawn closer to the Jewish experience of God. The Path is a process, like learning to play the piano. Generally, it takes time to develop and unfold, although sudden miraculous transformations can occur. As you work along the path, some aspects of *halakhah* will appeal to you, others will not. As you grow in Torah, more will begin to make sense to you. Your spiritual wisdom may have become eclipsed, but as your spiritual depths become part of your conscious awareness, you will feel God's presence more strongly each time you act with awareness of Torah's ideal.

Experience 17

A Sense of the Journey

Look back at your notes for each of the previous exercises in this book. Ask yourself if you've "really done it."

For the ones you haven't really done, ask yourself, Why not? Don't judge the answers, only ask them.

For the ones you have done, ask yourself, How am I different now from how I was before I did that exercise? What do I know now that I didn't know then?

Pay attention to these exercises as a path. Ask yourself whether you have a sense of where this path came from, or where it is leading you. Meditate on this question for several minutes. Let all the answers emerge without judgement.

❖

Chapter 5

Israel: Place, People and Polity

Like many other spiritual paths, the Jewish path contains a strong particularistic aspect. One place and one group of people are essential to the continuation of the path. Since the moment of its beginning, the Jewish spiritual path has been tied intimately to its sacred space, the Land of Israel, and to its community of adherents, the People of Israel.

Sacred Spaces

Certain places on earth facilitate spiritual experiences. Certain mountains, caves, groves, bodies of water, or simply designated spots, naturally inspire awe, humility and ecstasy. York, Chartres, Benares, Stonehenge, Maccu Pichu and Mecca retain this quality over centuries, even as the faith of their pilgrims changes.

Each salmon knows exactly which stream she came out of. At the end of her adult life, she swims to the spot of her origin to spawn and die. As with all archetypes, the holy place with which an individual resonates most deeply is determined at a very young age. Whether it is something intrinsic to the place which facilitates the experience, or something within the individual that is stimulated by awareness of place, is one of God's conundrums.

The sacred space is the "omphalos," the navel of the world,

85

where creation occurred and where the experience of God is most easily realized.

A visit to a sacred space is a pilgrimage. The importance of pilgrimage to the psyche is reflected in Islam's attitude toward pilgrimage to Mecca: it is deemed one of the five essential pillars of faith. Medieval Europe, no less than contemporary India, was well trodden with pilgrims. Pilgrimage is a metaphor for the inner spiritual journey.

Experience 18

Sensitizing Yourself to Holy Places

Choose a holy place to visit. It can be a natural place, such as a body of water, mountain or forest, or a place where humans have built something spiritual, such as a special synagogue, cathedral, memorial or tower. If nothing on this order is nearby, simply choose the highest or most desolate spot around.

Go to that place, alone, at a time when it is likely to be deserted. Spend an hour there, alone with yourself. Meditate, think about life, let your mind wander, reflect, pray, or else try to keep your mind free of all thought.

Pay attention to the special qualities of the place. Notice what special feelings or realizations are facilitated.

❖

Israel As Sacred Space

The Way of Torah is connected to *Erez Yisrael*, Land of

Israel, particularly Jerusalem and her Temple mount area, as its most sacred space. The Torah's Promised Land becomes the site of Solomon's Temple and its sacrifices, the longed for homeland during the sixty years of the first exile (586 BCE), and the longed for homeland throughout the 1900 years since the second Temple's destruction.

Throughout the unfolding of Jewish spirituality, Israel is not just a place. Israel is "Motherland" in the literal sense of the word: the fecund Earth who births her children. The Torah ascribes a special measure of God's love and protection to the Land of Israel: "It is a land on which *YHVH*, your God, always keeps an eye" (DEUTERONOMY 11: 12). The sages of the Talmud were so overcome with Israel's unique spiritual energy that they would kiss Israel's stones, mend her roads and lie down in her dust (B. KETUBBOT 112a). Seven hundred years ago, the sage Nachmanides wrote, "Torah can only be complete in the Land of Israel."

This yearning for Israel prompted numerous pilgrimages in ages when first-class travel meant three weeks on a donkey over rugged mountains, followed by a week on a dangerous, rat-infested galleon. Nachmanides also wrote that all the pain of separation from family and hardship of travel "are easy to bear...for it is agreeable to dwell even one day within Israel's precincts..."

For 1900 years, three of the daily *Tefillah's* nineteen benedictions request God's assistance in the reestablishment of the primordial period when all Jews experienced the glory of Jerusalem under Davidic kingship and received great influxes of spiritual energy from the daily Temple sacrifices. In addition, half of the Jewish holiday cycle celebrates Israel's agricultural year. Jews are buried with a clod of earth from the sacred space beneath their head, making literal the return to the Motherland's womb.

In modern times, a visit by a Jew to Israel is not simply a vacation, but a pilgrimage. In contemporary Jewish life, pilgrimage to Israel is commonly a transformative experience. Every rabbi has seen dozens of stories unfold where a Jew with no discernable spiritual connection goes on the pilgrimage and then redirects his or her life towards Jewish activities.

At a time when every square mile of this planet is endangered by ecological catastrophe, the reinforced connection of the heart and mind to one particular area stimulates a similar connection to the holiness of every other place on the face of Mother Earth.

Experience 19

A Connection to *Erez Yisrael,* the Land of Israel

Choose something you own (or aquire something if you don't have something) whose origin is the Land of Israel. Something very small is preferable. A piece of jewelry, a cheap tourist trinket, a small stone, a garment or a coin will do nicely.

Keep that item with you for an entire day. Hold the item in your hand at all times if possible. Wear it if it is a garment. Adapt your daily tasks in whatever way necessary so that you can keep the item in your hand and in your consciousness.

Throughout the day, whenever you become conscious of this item in your possession, direct your attention to your feelings about the Land of Israel.

Tribes

Since the dawn of civilization the tribe has been an essential human survival mechanism. We humans learned very early in our history that one individual or nuclear family is far more vulnerable than several dozen adults who band together.

The central features of an individual's life — language, culture, morals, social customs, religion and history — are functions of the tribe he/she belongs to. The manifestations of the archetypes are determined by one's tribe. Even "urban/suburban post-industrial America" has its own tribal characteristics, even though it includes millions of geographically diffused individuals whose common campfire is the television.

Many tribes have the notion that they have a particular task on earth.

The Tribe of Israel

The people of Israel constitute a tribe with shared origins and destiny, even if some commonalities usually found within tribes are absent. The archetypes of the Jewish collective unconscious are the same in Yemen, Norway, France, and North America. Jews throughout the world and throughout time resonate to the same spiritual practices.

Jews feel a tribal bond with one another. Jews recognize that Jews on the other side of the world are their not-so-distant thirty-second cousins. When two Jews from different cities meet, the typical opening conversation is a combing of memories for a common relative or aquaintance. For centuries Jewish travelers have been able to plug into the Jewish network in whatever distant city they find themselves.

As in an extended family, the tribal connective bond makes Jews rejoice for the success or grieve for the failures of fellow-Jews everywhere. Particularly when Jews somewhere are endangered, these feelings of interconnectedness become manifest.

One Jew's awareness that another Jew is her 32nd cousin is the underlying groundwork for her awareness that every fellow-human being in the world is her 132nd cousin.

The Jewish spiritual path depends upon a Jewish tribe which exercises that path and which is the vessel for the path's perpetuation. The 4000 year unbroken use of the path has been due to the empowering of the community by its experience of God. Particularly since the tribe of Israel has opted to remain a small minority, the strong tribal bond has allowed Torah to remain viable.

Membership in the tribe of Israel is often perceived as cultural or social and not necessarily spiritual. Membership in the tribe of Israel begs a large commitment of one's time and energy towards the diverse survival and support needs of the community. In major American cities it now offers cradle-to-grave social, cultural, and educational support institutions endowed by an absolutely fantastic philanthropic network. The Jewish family, replete with guilt inducing mother, though much maligned in recent years, has one strong argument in its favor: it has insured the continuity of the tribe amid generations of adverse circumstances. Though it may be stifling at times, it works better than anything else yet devised.

However, participation in Jewish social and cultural activities is an important component in the Way of Torah, rather than a substitute for it. The energy these activities demand and expend depends upon the energy evoked by the experience of God.

The tribe of Israel has always felt itself to have a special task on this plane, and membership in the tribe of Israel has always implied participation in this task. Israel's task is the continuation of the Covenant (Heb. *brit*). The Covenant was inaugurated at the time of Abraham's initial intuition of the Oneness of God. In the Covenantal agreement between Abraham and God, Abraham pledges that he and his clan will always affirm the Unity of God, and God pledges that Abraham's clan will survive against the harshest adversaries for millenia. The Torah records that when the Covenant was reaffirmed at Sinai, the souls of all Israelites ever to come were present (DEUTERONOMY 29: 14).

The 4000 year unbroken history of Israel implies a metaphysical reality to Israel's special task. The effect of maintaining that task is *tikkun olam*, the "Improvement of the World." The process of God's creation of the world is a continuing process in which the world is in a state of constant unfolding. As Torah becomes more manifest, the world becomes more spiritual, moving closer to God, its source. The manifest awareness of the Oneness of

God continues God's beginning of the creation of the world. "You" are God's partner in creation's continuity.

Living within the Way of Torah and the tribe of Israel breaks the limitations of this lifetime. Notions of afterlife get relatively little Jewish attention and very few individuals' personal creations survive much beyond their years. The primary Jewish thrust for immortality is the immortality achieved through the continuity of this most ancient tribe whose effect on the world has been so considerable. By working for the perpetuation of the Jewish tribe and by bearing and raising children who will continue that work, one lives beyond this incarnation. In the Talmud's words, "You are not obligated to complete the work, but neither are you free to ignore it" (M. AVOT 2:16).

Experience 20

Your Great-Grandmother's Great-Grandfather/
Your Distant Jewish Ancestor

This visualization experience will connect you to a Jewish ancestor from your distant past. If you know that "your great-grandmother's greatgrandfather" or some similar relative was Jewish, then use this experiment with the words in parentheses () and skip the bracketed [] words. If you can identify no such direct Jewish ancestor, then substitute the bracketed words. If you doubt that you had a distant Jewish ancestor, then suspend that doubt for the length of this exercise.

Enter a state of deep relaxation as you did in the experience of meeting one of your archetypes (page 8). When you enter that "dimly lit corridor," segué into the following:

On one of the doorways you will find a sign that says, (Your great-grandmother's great-grandfather) [Your distant Jewish ancestor]. Experience yourself slowly opening that doorway...and there you can experience your great-grandmother's great-grandfather [your distant Jewish ancestor]. Imagine what he or she looked like. Picture the clothing and the place this person lived in. Hear the sounds of the environment. Observe your ancestor going about daily tasks...See your ancestor in synagogue. Listen to him daven. Acknowledge your feelings about him or her.

Initiate a conversation. Introduce yourself...Tell why you've come to visit. Tell how you feel about meeting. Let him tell you how he feels about meeting you...Tell what you've received from him. Let your ancestor respond. Tell your ancestor what's most important to you. Let him respond. If you have a gift, give it to him. Maybe he has a gift to give you.

You're going to leave in a moment. If there is anything more you'd like to say or to ask you can do so now. Your ancestor can respond. You can return to speak further some other time if you wish. Your ancestor will still be here. Say goodbye now. And when you are ready, return to the room.

❖

The State of Israel and Sacred Space

The modern State of Israel derives from the experience of the Land of Israel as sacred space for the tribe of Israel while performing her task. Zionism, the process that created the State of Israel, is a politicization of the tribal spiritual experience. Zionism's ability to create a state so modern, so quickly from the ashes of the Holocaust indicates the depth and power of that spiritual underpinning. Throughout the State's history, her diverse successes have made the intensity of the connection to sacred space transfer quite easily to the political entity.

In the contemporary rendition of the Jewish myth, the precariousness of Jewish survival reached new heights under Nazi Germany, and the State of Israel is essential for continued Jewish physical survival. In addition, the State itself is *rayshit ge'ulateinu*, the first step in an ongoing process of tribal redemption.

The State of Israel's actions elicit strong reactions from Jews. Her support is virtually automatic. Even when the State's actions are difficult to defend, most Jews are loath to acknowledge the fact in public and when a few do, most others are uncomfortable.

The hard reality of the world is that Jews' physical survival has never been something to be taken for granted. By drawing upon the power of the Land's sacredness and intensifying it, the State of Israel has assumed much of the tribe's responsibility for the physical safety of its members.

Unfortunately, the Arab states' inability to accept the existence of a Jewish state among them has created a forty-two year defensive seige. One of the worst effects of the Arabs' rejection of Israel has been Israel's resultant inability to recognize the emerging reality of the Palestinian people. Ironically, this chain of cause and effect creates the perception that Israel, the only true democracy in the Middle East, is a villianous oppressor. Yet within the psyche of Jews today a nagging fear will not totally evaporate that the tribe of Palestinian Arabs are, in fact, reflections of ourselves in more ways than we care to enumerate. Until a political settlement unfolds, balancing respect for ones enemy with the self-respect that keeps us alive is an extra task in the spiritual life that demands an expenditure of energy in this real, material world.

The Jew's connection to the State of Israel binds together the Land of Israel and the People of Israel. However, as most of the world's Jews choose not to live there, the primordial connection has not been superseded by its politicization.

Chapter 6

The Experience of God

The experience of God is the ultimate, peak human experience. It is tremendous and wonderful, a phenomenon which puts all other life experiences into proper perspective.

The experience of God is one which most humans yearn to have. Many people are willing to give up a great deal to reach it. Some will even sacrifice all other human goals—fame, fortune, family, knowledge and excitement—to achieve it.

Most everyone perceives a hint of awe or numinosity from time to time. People often describe a day walking in the woods or at the ocean as being somehow closer to God. The "experience of God," however, connotes something greater, more unusual, more overpowering. Very few people have such an experience more than a few moments of a lifetime.

There is a misguided tendency within Jewish scholarship to relegate all descriptions of the experience of God, as well as the paranormal, to a particular category called "Jewish mysticism" or "the *Kabbalah*" ("what has been received"). However, the books which are usually ascribed to that category, such as the *Zohar, Sefer Yezirah*, and the Hasidic literature are part of the Jewish whole. These works are no less essential to Judaism's mainstream than the Talmud, and their authors are no more or less "mystic" than the authors of the Talmud's "legalism."

The experience of God is neither regression to preconscious infant experience, nor an acute psychotic event. Like both of those, it involves breaking the ego's normal boundaries and altering the distinction between self and other. However, it is also a distinct experience unto itself.

There is a Jewish path to that experience, facilitated by the spiritual insights of Torah and the directed action of *halakhah*. However, any human experience is perceived through the body. The experience of God is no different. All sensations are perceived, all emotions are felt, and thoughts realized, in and by the body.

Without the body as the central point of organization, all human experience as we know it would not possible. Even reported "out of body" experiences involve "leaving" and "returning to" the body.

In most respects, we are no different from our ancestors who lived 5000 years ago. While our range of knowledge and experience exceeds their reality or imagination, in the deepest, most essential sense we remain the same. On the *nefesh* level, little has changed. Our bodies are identical to their bodies, our emotional make up is relatively the same. We feel love and anger, security and fear, compassion and violence, just as they did. Our hunger to learn and grow is much the same. While our intellect is more developed, we go through the same process of developing our natural talents. We are born knowing nothing, and spend our lives acquiring knowledge.

On the *ru'aḥ* level, not much has changed either. We still need a guide to moral and ethical action, just as they did. For instance, medical technology has made ethical decisions far more complex — and necessary — as we confront the issues of organ donations, surrogate parenting, the rights of the unborn child.

On the *neshamah* level, change has also been minimal. The basic drive to reunite with the Source of all life is as strong as it has ever been. Since Abraham intuited the Unity of God, our advances in technology have not made the quest for God much easier or quicker. Sacred technology is, for the most part, very ancient. Prayer, meditation, dream interpretation, celebration and oracle have only evolved minimally in thousands of years.

The Physiology of God

Any human experience can be described in terms of the changes it produces in the body. The experience of stage fright, for instance, is a variety of physical tensions in the muscles. The muscular tension is what the performer feels and calls "fear." The experience of "love" is the name we give to a specific set of physiological responses: quickening heartbeat, increased adrenaline flow, heightened sensual and sexual responses.

The experience of God has a set of very subtle but real physiological responses which accompany it. These have been identified and described through the ages by different sacred technicians of various cultures.

In India and China, the physiological structures which are effected by the experience of God are called *chakras*. In Judaism they are *sephirot*.

Chakras and *Sephirot*

The Indian *chakras* (Sanskrit for "centers") and Jewish *sephirot* (literally, "spheres") are essentially the same, although there are differences between the two systems.

Each system describes the inner workings of the "God experience." They answer the question: "What happens in your mind and body when that experience unfolds?"

The *chakra* system emphasizes the internal experience, while the *sephirot* emphasizes the physically transcendent, metaphysical nature of reality. In both systems the alchemical dictum applies: "As above, so below." The internal human map is an exact replica of the external universal map.

Our Western orientation tends to rely on laboratory experimentation to learn what is happening to an organism. But the experience of God is rare and illusive. It is unpredictable and defies patterns of cause and effect.

In the East, intuitive, introspective physiological observation is taken seriously. Eastern medicine considers a variety of energies which Western science hasn't yet observed, much less studied. For example, acupuncture is still a curiosity in the West, whereas in China it's been used for centuries. In the West, because its claims have not been measured, it is not yet considered a valid healing tool.

Eastern physiology recognizes seven energy centers located in the body. Called *chakras*, they are psychic sense organs, the places where the sensation of energy is concentrated in any human experience. These *chakras* are mapped in a "lower to higher" configuration, with the lowest *chakra* found in the base of the spine. The second *chakra* is at either the spleen or the genitals, the third at the navel, the fourth at the heart region. The fifth *chakra* lies at the throat, the sixth is between the eyebrows (the "third eye"), and the seventh sits right at the crown of the head. There is no system of identifiable anatomic structures in Western medicine which correspond to these seven locations.

At any given moment, our psychological and physiological states can be described by evaluating the levels of vital energy at each *chakra*. In the normal resting state, our energy is concentrated at the three lower *chakras*. As we progress physically, emotionally, mentally and spiritually closer to God, the vital energies shift their concentration to the higher *chakras*.

This vital energy is called *kundalini* (Sanskrit, "serpent power"). It is usually described as a coiled snake which dwells in the lowest *chakra*, waiting to be awakened. Through yoga, meditation, chanting, exercise and other spiritual disciplines, the *kundalini* rises up the path of the spine, filling the higher *chakras* and opening new levels of human experience. Raising the *kundalini* is the psycho-physiological key to increased consciousness, and ultimately the experience of God.

The Four Lower *Chakras*

The lowest *chakra*, the *muladhara*, holds the energy needed for locomotion. It is described as a disc of red light and is located at the coccyx or base of the spine. It is the center of energy needed to meet the basic physical needs to move, to gather food, to escape danger.

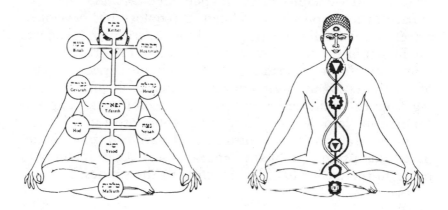

The parallel structure of the *sephirot* shown on the left, and the location of the *chakras* on the right. (Source: Kabbalah, *Charles Ponce, Straight Arrow Books*)

The second *chakra*, the *swadhisthana*, controls sexual drive and is described as a disc of vermillion light. After meeting basic survival needs, the next most important need is preserving the species.

The third *chakra*, the *manipura*, is the center of the ego drive, the will and desire for power and mastery. Located at the navel, it is a disc of blue or green light. In the Japanese adaptation of the *chakra* system, it is called the hara and is essential for balance, strength and grace in the martial arts. Our inclinations to lead and rule, to build and be in control, are aspects of the *manipura*.

The fourth *chakra*, the *anahata*, is the seat of compassion, love and unselfishness. Located between the two nipples, it controls the heart and is perceived as a disc of red or golden light. It accounts for the feeling of "falling in love" as well as compassion, when "one heart goes out to another." Altruism and religious values are experienced in the fourth *chakra*. It is the gateway between the physical energies of the lower three *chakras* and the more spiritual energies of the higher three *chakras*.

Each major approach of Western psychology has developed a deep understanding of one piece of the *chakra* map. Freud was the master of the second *chakra*. He saw all unresolved human conflict and feeling as extensions of sexuality. Adler was a master of the third *chakra*, interpreting all human problems as resulting from ego deficiencies and inferiority complexes. Jung was the first modern Western thinker to probe into the subtleties of the experiences of the fourth through seven *chakras*. He believed that psychic problems were the result of our inability to relate to the archetypal ideal intrinsic to the species.

Experience 21

Becoming Aware of the First Four *Chakras*

1) Find a comfortable, quiet place where you will not be disturbed. Use whatever techniques best help you to relax very deeply and to focus your awareness within.

2) Imagine yourself walking or running, as quickly and gracefully as possible. Then focus your attention on the base of your spine. Feel the energy that is concentrated there. Notice that in your mind's eye you accelerate as soon as your attention is focused on this *chakra*. (Try this shift in focus the next time you are actually running or walking. You may experience real physi-

cal acceleration.)

3) Shift the focus of your awareness to your sexuality and give yourself permission to concentrate on it for a few moments. Allow yourself to use whatever sexual fantasy you desire to feel your sexuality radiating from your genitalia throughout your body.

4) Shift your awareness to your navel. Allow yourself to experience a desire for power and mastery. Feel the desire to possess and to consume. Does this bring up specific memories? Notice how desire centers at the stomach, and how similar willfullness feels to hunger.

5) Shift your awareness to your heart. Allow yourself to feel unconditional love. Feel the desire to move closer to a beloved person in your life. Notice if this stirs up memories of falling in love, being in love or of heartbreak.

❖

The Three Higher *Chakras*

The fifth *chakra*, the *vishuddha*, is located at the thyroid gland in the center of the throat. It is most frequently experienced as a "lump in the throat" signifying intense, overflowing love and compassion. It is also activated at those moments where "we don't know whether to laugh or cry." The *vishudda* is perceived as a disc of violet light. Its energy controls the respiratory and auditory sensations, and it also allows for extrasensory perception, psychic ability and intuition.

The sixth *chakra*, the *ajna*, is located between the eyebrows, in the place often portrayed in Eastern art as the "third eye". Perceived as a disc of intense white light, it controls all higher intellectual functions and is felt to control the secretions of the pituitary gland. Energizing the sixth *chakra* also causes the experience of the "astral body," the pure consciousness which is only loosely attached to the physical body. The experience of the "guru within," "spirit guide," or "guardian angel" comes from sixth *chakra* energy.

The seventh *chakra*, the *sahasrara*, is located at the crown of the head, or a few inches above. It is activated at moments of highest experience of the Oneness of God. Connected to the pineal gland this center is said to have control over every aspect of the body and mind. Energy from this center is perceived as the "Great White Light." This light atop the head of highly spiritual individuals is depicted as halos in Western artwork.

The purpose of yoga, meditation and other Eastern spiritual practices is to raise the *kundalini* from the lower to highest *chakras*. This is difficult because of the body's physical armor. Tension in the muscles pinch off the flow of energy up the spine. Usually, raising the energy requires a deliberate physical, as well as spiritual, discipline. Yoga stretches the muscles to break up the dams that restrict flow. Breath control relaxes the muscles. Meditation focuses attention so that physical distress can fade.

The *Sephirot*

As with the *chakras*, the *sephirot* designate energy centers in the body. There are ten *sephirot*. The third, fifth and sixth *chakras* each translate into two *sephirot*, a complimentary pair of harmonious opposites. The *chakras* are usually delineated from the lowest to the highest. The *sephirot* are usually counted from the top down.

The *sephirot* are frequently depicted in the pattern of *adam kadmon*, "archetypal human." *Adam kadmon* is both the blueprint for all other human beings and also the metaphysical pattern of the universe. The *sephirot* in this configuration are referred to as the archetypal tree of life, the *etz ḥayim*.

The highest *sephirah* (singular for *sephirot*), *keter*, "infinity" sits at the crown of *adam kadmon's* head and corresponds directly to the seventh *chakra*. It represents God's Essence, the "Oneness-of-All." It can be experienced but its mystery can never be understood. Even the experience is only a hint of an Infinity beyond the realm of human experience.

The second and third *sephirot*, *hokhmah* and *binah*, correspond to the sixth *chakra*. Placed at *adam kadmon's* right and left brain hemispheres, they are the primary qualities that pervade all the universe. *Hokhmah* is masculine, *yang,* active, pure abstract power. *Binah* is feminine, *yin,* receptive, pure intuitive power. They sit on the opposite temples, balancing each other in harmonious opposition.

The fourth and fifth *sephirot*, *hesed* and *gevurah*, correspond to the fifth *chakra*. They are also a pair in dynamic harmony, at either sides of the throat. *Hesed* is God's nurturing love, but it sits beneath *hokhmah*. *Gevurah* is the power of God to move one to action, but it sits on the side of *binah*. *Hesed* and *gevurah* evolve from *hokhamah* and *binah* while they involve their opposites in their synthesis. Abraham and Sarah personify *hesed;* Isaac and Rebecca personify *gevurah*.

The sixth *sephirah*, *tiferet*, rests at the heart. It synthesizes *hesed* and *gevurah* into the experience of God as a "You," who can be approached and communicated with. *Tiferet* is both a funnel and synthesis between the purely metaphysical *sephirot* above and the more earthly *sephirot* below. *Tiferet* is stimulated by the experience of the archetypes. Jacob/Rachel/Leah are *Tiferet* personified.

The seventh and eigth *sephirot*, *nezah* and *hod*, are another pair. Jointly corresponding to the third *chakra*, *nezah* is "dominance" and *hod*, "submissiveness." They are usually depicted at either hip. As they are more enmeshed in the material world, they represent experiences which are more familiar to everyday life. At this level the harmonious opposites sometimes struggle together.

The ninth *sephirah*, *yesod*, correspond to the genital *chakra*. Although the figure of *adam kadmon* is usually masculine and *yesod* is located at the penis, occasionally *yesod* is a fig leaf, denoting an androgynous character. Like *tiferet* directly above it, *yesod* synthesizes the higher realms and funnels them. Thus, *yesod* is the gateway to the spiritual realm from the material. *Yesod's* dynamic force impregnates *malkhut* below.

The lowest *sephirah*, *malkhut*, translates to "God's kingdom," that is, the physical world which contains hints of the spiritual realm. Although *malkhut* is inert and lifeless without an infusion of spiritual energy from above, it is included in the fullness of God. This *sephirah* is also identified with *Shekhinah*, ("proximity"). *Shekhinah*, a common Jewish name for God, usually stresses God's feminine, immanent aspects. Thus, God in the physical world is dependent on the spiritual activity of humanity for God's spiritual process to unfold.

Experience 22

Recognizing *Sephirot* in Your Body

1) Find a quiet, comfortable place and relax.

2) Begin with the lowest *sephirah*, *malkhut*. Concentrate awareness on your feet. Focus your attention on the essential quality of receptivity.

3) Move your attention upward to the second *sephirah*, *yesod* or sexuality, located at the genitals. Keep your attention fixed for several minutes.

4) Move your attention upward to the opposing pairs of *nezah* and *hod*. *Nezah* at the right hip is the quality of dominance. *Hod* at the left hip is subservience.

5) Proceed upward, concentrating on the quality of *tiferet*, beauty, at the heart. Continue to the pair of *gevurah*, strength, at the left shoulder and *hesed*, love at the right shoulder. Continue to focus your awareness on *binah*, intuition, at the left side

of the brain, and *hokhmah*, logic, on the right side of the brain. Finally, concentrate on *keter*, infinity, just above the head.

❖

The *Sephirot* and Metaphysics

The *sephirot* structure has three levels of meaning. *Keter* on on the high end, *malkhut* at the base, indicate gradations in a continuum. First, it explains how God and humans are different ends of the same spectrum. Second, it concretizes the intuition that God is both transcendant and immanent and many shades in between. Third, it indicates that our experiences of God are not the true reality of God. A simplistic reading of the Torah might indicate that God and human are separate from one another, that God is only experienced as transcendent, and that what Israel experienced at Sinai was all that God is. A simplistic view of metaphysics might be that the human is God, that God is totally immanent, and that what we experience is all that God is. The *sephirot* mediate these two extremes.

The *sephirot* are part of every human experience. In an extreme form, a victim of a serious accident recovers and the next of kin experience *hesed*, God's loving nurturance. That same victim dies, and the next of kin are consoled with an awareness of *gevurah*, God's justice. In a less extreme form, an experience of the beauty of a leaf's veins is an expression of *tiferet* acting upon *malkhut*. An awareness of the fundamental interaction of qualities in the universe, the dance of *yin* and *yang*, is an awareness of *hokhmah* and *binah*, the right and left of *adam kadmon*.

Tantra

Eastern and Jewish traditions both draw their inspiration from
the same universal archetypes. They translate archetypal intuitions into the symbology of their respective pasts. One Eastern
variation on the use of *chakras* is Tantra.

Tantra is a hidden, esoteric part of the Hindu and Buddhist
traditions and is often denounced by their orthodox teachers.
Like more familiar aspects of these traditions, Tantra's teachings
describe how to experience God through raising energy from the
lowest *chakras* to the highest. However, some of its techniques
involve sexual activities.

According to Tantra, the universe and everything in it is permeated by a secret power, emanating from the single Source of
all Being. This power manifests itself in three forms: receptive
inertia (female power), dynamic energy (male power), and the
harmonious union of the two. These three forms of one power
underlie every movement in the universe and every activity in
the human organism.

Through rites and rituals, the Tantric practitioner experiences
the *chakras* in his or her body and identifies them with the *chakras*
of the universe, and the male/female polarity in God.

In Tantra, everything in creation is divided into positive and
negative, male and female, passive and kinetic, electric and mag-
netic energies. Every man and woman embodies a dominant side
of the secret, fundamental forces that control the universe. In
order to experience God, the Tantric must, literally, join him
or herself to the opposite manifestation of this force. When an
intense physical union occurs between a male-electrical dominated individual and a female-magnetic dominated individual,
the couple provide a conduit for cosmic force, which flows
through them and into the earth. Thus, sexual intercourse is a
serious religious ritual to facilitate the experience of God.

In Tantra, sexual intercourse is practiced as meditation. Tantric texts are often "how to" sex manuals. However, rather than
concentrating on pleasure, they detail the mental states to be

achieved during sexual activity. The Tantric sexual act is a long, deliberate process requiring control of thought, breath and movement. Tantra maintains that properly channeled sexual activity is the fastest and most direct process for raising the *kundalini* up through the *chakras*. In other words, Tantra transform sexual activity into spiritual experience.

The object of Tantric sex is not to discharge primal lust, or even to make love in the usual sense of the term, but rather to participate in the essential male/female polarity of God. Nor is Tantric activity restricted to married partners. Tantric societies have religious functionaries, skilled in techniques which they teach their students.

From the vantage point of Torah, Tantra may seem to be blasphemy, an abomination. Torah restricts virtually all acceptable sexual expression to marriage. Judaism does not make a common practice of describing specific sexual activities, particularly as a means of experiencing God. Torah specifically forbids Tantra-like sexual rituals (DEUTERONOMY 23:18) which were common to ancient Israel's neighboring cultures. According to one *aggadah*, the *Tanakh's* 1000 year long struggle between Israelite monotheism and the Canaanite polytheism it supplanted was due to the Israelites' infatuation with Canaanite sexual rituals. Although a great deal of the Talmud is concerned with sexually related matters, its tone is clinical and its attitude far less than celebratory.

Yet, on closer examination, Torah and Tantra share common insights. Judaism accepts sexuality as a normal part of human existence and Torah recognizes the immense spiritual power which can be experienced through sexuality. An entire section of *aggadah* literature is devoted to interpreting the spiritual meaning of the *Tanakh's* Song of Songs, which appears to be erotic love poetry. At least one Jewish classic from the 13th century, called the Holy Letter (*Iggeret Ha-kodesh*) propounds a rich view of sexuality as a Divine creation. It states that "sexuality can be a means of spiritual elevation when it is properly practiced, and the mystery greater than this is that secret celestial couplings unite according to a male-female pattern."[1]

Like Tantra, the *sephirot* system indicates that the human being is a replica of the universe. Both systems are aware that there
is a male / female polarity active within the unities of the universe,
the individual, and God, and that their conjunction is essential
for any kind of growth.

The conjunction of male and female is also of utmost importance because the *neshamah* of each individual has both male
and female aspects. Prior to birth, the *neshamah* unites male
and female aspects into one undifferentiated whole. At conception, however, the *neshamah* is divided into male and female
parts which then take residence in separate bodies. Sexual union is the means to the restoration to primal wholeness of two
halves. It is the act of returning to one's state of origin.

Torah does have a ritual sexual activity which serves to unite
man and woman with God as they unite with each other, and
this is the ritual of sexual union on *Shabbat*. Sexual expression
between husband and wife is actually demanded by one of the
613 *mizvot* of the Torah. The *halakhah* specifies minimal
frequency of intercourse, usually once a week but adjusted for
age, health, occupation, desire and time spent away from home.
There is also the strong recommendation that the sexual act take
place on Friday night, the eve of *Shabbat*.

The interplay of the *sephirot* embodies a male / female polarity. *Malkhut*, the material world, is feminine and is identified
with *Shekhinah*, the feminine, immanent aspects of God. The
other nine sephirot are collectively *Kadosh Barukh Hu*, the Holy
Blessed One, which is male. On the eve of Shabbat, the transition from male to female takes place within God. The first six
days of the week are masculine-active, but on *Shabbat* the
feminine-receptive predominates. At midnight on Friday night,
the male and female become united within God in perfect un-

---

[1] Nachmanides (ascribed), *Igeret Hakodesh*, The Holy Letter. S. Cohen, editor. New York:
KTAV, 1978, p. 48 (author's translation).

differentiated wholeness. By imitating God and uniting male and female, humans have the opportunity to participate in the ultimate experience.

In addition, this union of male and female is reflected in other aspects of Torah as well. A 16th century meditation that precedes the performance of *mizvot* is included in many prayerbooks: "I am ready and prepared to fulfill this *mizvah* in order to unify the Holy Blessed One and his *Shekhinah* by means of that which is most subtle and hidden within each Israelite."

Jung's description of the spiritual growth process, what he calls the process of individuation, involves three central aspects: the recognition and assimilation of the shadow energy; recognition and assimilation of the energy of the anima, for men, and the animus, for women; and the emergence of the Self. The shadow, roughly equivalent to Freud's *id*, represents repressed unacceptable desires. The animus or anima is the sexually opposite mirror image of oneself, what the man or the woman would have been had each been born the opposite sex. The animus/anima forms the image of the opposite-sex god/goddess within that we project onto every lover and opposite-sex archetype. Its recognition and the reassimilation of its energy unleashes immense transformational experience. The Self is the Higher Self, or the *neshamah*.

Both Torah and Tantra provide a map for the immensely powerful reassimilation of the animus/anima and the experience of the emergence of the Self. This experience is perceived as the universal, archetypal, most intense experience of God.

Chapter 7

Patriarchy and Matriarchy

A child's first image of God is almost always an old man with a white beard on a throne up in the clouds. It is rarely an old woman with a white shawl over her head up in those clouds. Our first image of God is a predominant archetype throughout our entire life.

The oldest forms of spiritual and social organization on earth were matriarchies. Traditional matriarchal spiritualities were tied to one place where the everpresent mysteries of nature were celebrated.

Universal patriarchy supplanted matriarchy due to a shift in the mythological structure along with its early technological and material successes. The snowballing patriarchal process worldwide has only recently begun to be redirected, due to another shift in the archetypal structure along with women's effective utilization of the fruits of that technology.

Patriarchy and Torah

The transition from matriarchy to patriarchy occurred about 4000 years ago, about the same time that the Jewish path began. Early patriarchal systems were more easily transported from one locale to another. Abraham's experience of God led him on a journey away from his birthplace. Thus, the transition to patriarchy corresponds to emigration, and is tied into the beginnings of the Jewish path.

For the last several thousand years, the great majority of all the people of the world have participated in patriarchal spiritual paths. If Judaism has not been less rigid and oppressive in its patriarchy than most, at least it has been no worse.

The Torah's creation tale is ambivalent about women. The equality of man and woman is suggested in the first side of the creation myth (GENESIS 1:26), while woman is derivative from man in the second (GENESIS 2:22). Though both man and woman are punished and expelled from Paradise for succumbing to the serpent, the woman is henceforth to be ruled by her husband. Christian exegesis of this story has derived from it woman's essential blame for gullibility and coercion of her mate. Torah's understanding, however, hears it say the two share the consequences more or less equally.

One archetype to emerge in the *aggadah* of Creation is Lilith. The name of this ancient Babylonian goddess is transposed into the woman who God created as Adam's coequal. When she demands Adam treat her as equal sexually and spiritually, he refuses and she leaves. Living alone in the wilderness, she becomes the temptress of all men and the jealous witch who steals the babies that she cannot bear. It is only after Lilith's departure that Eve is created out of Adam in the second aspect of creation. Although Lilith has hardly been held up as a role model for women and her power is viewed as demonic, her myth still acknowledges women's primeval equality with men.

Torah focuses on the saga of the founding fathers, not the matriarchs. However, the women are present and active throughout the Torah. Furthermore, like their male counterparts, they are archetypes, universal and in many ways larger than life.

The Talmud is divided into six major subdivisions, each of which is several volumes long and dedicated to one central area of study. One of these sections is called "Women" (*nashim*).

However, the Talmud was written by men for men. The Rabbis who shaped it mention they consulted with their wives only occasionally.

The spiritual and secular leadership of Judaism has always been almost exclusively male. The male prophets, scribes, rabbis, judges, teachers and political leaders have rarely allowed a female colleague. Nevertheless, there have been a few notable exceptions: Moses' sister, Miriam, was a prophet. Deborah and Esther were important heroic leaders. The wives of several preeminent rabbis of the Talmud were great scholars.

The patriarchal predominance in leadership is so great that writers of sacred texts have deliberately avoided discussing how women have experienced God. Most often, such descriptions are seen through male characters, be they natural or historic events, or psychic phenomena. Again, there are notable exceptions. Rebecca inquires of the meaning of her uncomfortable pregnancy (GENESIS 25:22), Miriam leads the newly freed women in song and dance (EXODUS 15:20), and Hannah prays ecstatically (I SAMUELS 1-2:10).

Torah has limited women's civil rights and power. Under Torah's civil law, women cannot be witnesses in court, sign contracts or initiate a divorce. But if at her own wedding, a woman's only activity is to accept her groom's invitation to be his wife, at least her free acquiescence was required and her act of "accepting" was her method of signing a contract. A woman's property may be subject to her husband's or father's supervision, but she does retain some rights over it.

Another example of the patriarchal predominance of Torah is its language of God, which is male. Hebrew verbs, nouns and pronouns are masculine or feminine. When Torah talks about God, or Jews talk to God, the masculine forms are almost always used. Even though God is supposed to unite both male and female, the message is clear.

The Goddess Asherah

In support of the premise that *YHVH* unites male and female, the Jewish God, unlike all others in the ancient Near East, has no consort and engages in no sexual activity. This was a revolutionary idea in its time, and was very slow to be accepted even in ancient Israel.

The Torah repeatedly commands the Israelites to destroy the indigenous Canaanite cults. These cults had very strong goddess components. While the Torah finds these spiritual paths abhorrent, archeologic evidence and the *Tanakh's* own historic account suggest the Israelites found them fascinating.

The 800 years of Israelite history recorded in the Prophetic Books were characterized by the struggle between separate male and female images of God, versus one undifferentiated God. Official Israelite spirituality insisted upon the Oneness of God. However, attraction to a female component of God was so strong that devotion to the goddess Asherah became a popular movement. She was even venerated with a sacred monument inside the Temple of Jerusalem during most of those 800 years. Figurines of Asherah are one of the most commonly found archaeological remnants of ancient Israel.[1]

The prophets and scribes who edited the prophetic books were unshakable in their belief that any reference to the feminine side of God must not allow multiple gods. While Asherah might have been excused as a misunderstanding of the feminine side of God, because she was seen as an independent goddess her worship was condemned.

Some female images of God can be found in the Tanakh. Besides the predominant male images of a warrior (EXODUS 15: 3), a deliverer (EXODUS 15:13) and a law-giver (EXODUS 19:18), God is also depicted as Israel's mother: "Didn't I conceive this people? Did I birth them?" (NUMBERS 12:11). The prophet Isaiah was par-

---

[1] R. Patai. *The Hebrew Goddess*. New York: KTAV, 1967, p. 36-50.

ticularly fond of this image: "As one is comforted by his mother, so I will comfort you." (ISAIAH 66:13). The 22nd Psalm refers to God as a midwife: "You are the One who took me from the womb; you kept me safe on my mother's breast" (PSALMS 22:9).

As a result of Asherah's controversial history, the path of Torah has never facilitated the experience of God as "She." The *Shekhinah* is a familiar name of God which emphasizes God's female aspects: near and available, compassionate, receptive. However, the name *Shekhinah* is noticeably absent from davening.

Even when appealing to God's compassion during davening, the appeal is made to "Our Father, Our King" (*Heb. Avenu Malkeinu*), never "Our Mother, Our Queen" (*Heb. Imeinu Malkateinu*). A request in the Yom Kippur liturgy that God relate to us "as a mother bird flutters over her children" is a conspicuous exception, as is the previously mentioned 16th century meditation that performance of a *mizvah* unites The Holy Blessed One with his *Shekhinah*.

One particularly irritating line which begins the morning davening praises God "for not having made me a woman." The correlative line for women praises God "who has made me according to his will." Although this line has been expurgated from most recent prayerbooks, the fact that it hasn't totally disappeared is symptomatic of Torah's patriarchal tendencies. (When davening from an unexpurgated prayerbook, one can amend these lines to a positive statement, praising God for "having made me a man or a woman.")

The process of re-owning female images of the One God is still in its early stages. It is one of the most significant processes to unfold in the Jewish spiritual world in 4000 years.

Experience 23

Praying to God as Male or Female

1) Get a daily *siddur* (prayerbook). Find the prayer called
"*Avenu Malkeinu*," "Our Father, Our King" at the conclusion
of the daily Afternoon (*minḥah*) service. It consists of a long list of
supplications, each beginning with "*Avenu Malkeinu.*"
2) Spend a few moments preparing yourself for prayer.
3) Pray *Avenu Malkeinu*, in Hebrew or English.
4) Repeat this exercise, but change the words to "*Imeinu
Malkateinu*," Our Mother, Our Queen.
5) Compare your experience of the two prayers.

❖

Women and Rituals

Throughout most of Jewish history, women have not had the
opportunity to study Torah, nor been able to perform most of
the *miẓvot*. *Halakhah's* and *aggadah's* spiritual practices have not
been available to women. In its negative sense, this implies that
women are bound to a domestic role whose obligations take prece-
dence over the spiritual, or that they are incapable of lofty spiritual achievement. In the positive sense, it might imply that women's
natural spiritual talents make the other *miẓvot* superfluous.

Until about 150 years ago, every synagogue segregated wom-
en behind a dividing barrier (*meḥiẓah*), while men performed
virtually every aspect of the davening and public rituals. About
one-third of synagogues (the Orthodox) maintain this rigid sexual separation. Although this pattern does foster solidarity and
emotional closeness among both women and men, one can hardly

hold it up a paradigm of protofeminism. Within more liberal Jewish movements, the "egalitization" of the rituals has been unmistakable if gradual.

Three *mizvot* have been traditionally designated especially for women. Women inaugurate *Shabbat* by lighting candles. Light symbolizes spiritual light which is present throughout the material world. For most Jews, the memory of their grandmother lighting *Shabbat* candles is powerful and profound.

Preparing food and setting aside a piece for God is one of humanity's most ancient spiritual acts. Women continue the practice by separating a pinch of dough while kneading the *ḥallah*, the special twisted egg bread eaten to inaugurate *Shabbat*. It is one of the remnants of the sacrificial system, the tap-root of all Jewish spirituality.

Women and Sexuality

The third *mizvah* of women is called *taharat hamishpaḥah*, "family purity." It is the one *mizvah* that sums up in itself the whole spectrum of sexuality and relationships. In recent times, it has received bad press and deserves a re-examination.

Sexuality and spirituality are commonly perceived to be on opposite ends of the spectrum of human experience. Sex is physical, material, temporal, and can induce guilt. Spirit is clean, pure, close to God. The Jewish spiritual path, like Tantra, argues that on a certain level, sexuality and spirituality come together, both on Earth and in God, and that merging of the two becomes most complete on *Shabbat* eve.

American culture has a deep ambivalence about sexuality. Its dominant Protestant spiritual lineage has its roots in the strongly anti-sexual Puritanism of England. This attitude went virtually unchallenged through the 1950's. During the last twenty-five years, the pendulum has swung. A part of American culture has adopted an ethic that regards sexual restraint as unhealthy.

Since AIDS has entered our vocabulary, that ambivalence has

become even more pronounced, as we now fear illness, amidst the other confusion. This ambivalence is particularly clear each time a well known clergy-person admits to sexual misconduct. Some are shocked, while defenders will argue that their leader was set up by his enemies. Others feel vindicated and bemoan the hypocrisy of religion.

A broader based perspective on sexuality would start with the admission that sexuality and spiritually are different manifestations of the same basic human energy. A statement in the *midrash* literature acknowledges, "the greater the man, the stronger his sexuality" (LEVITICUS RABBAH 26:5). A central task on the spiritual path is to transform sexual energy into spiritual energy.

Every major religious tradition recognizes that harnessing the power of sexual energy is essential for spiritual development. The dominant thread running through Christian tradition regards all sexual expression as unfortunately necessary while intrinsically evil. Christianity regards sexual abstinence, or in some cases celibacy, as essential to spiritual growth.

On the other end of the spectrum, Taoist tradition in China and the Tantric tradition in India allow for sexual expression as part of spiritual work. Tantra has developed a "Yoga of Sex" which goes so far as to prescribe specific sexual activities to facilitate spiritual growth, which from Western perspective might seem titillating, if not pornographic.

The more common varieties of Buddhism and Hinduism prescribe sexual abstinence as an important part of spiritual growth, or they allow the cultivation of pleasure as one part of the path of God, rather than the sole focus.

Torah and *halakhah* have an approach to sexuality which is somewhere between Tantric and Christian extremes. *Halakhah* recognizes an essential goodness to sexuality and it avoids attitudes which incline toward abstinence. Anyone drawn to sexual abstinence would have a difficult time on Torah's path. *Halakhah* specifies a minimal frequency of sexual intercourse that is required. Sexual intercourse is, in fact, a devotional activity.

However, *halakhah* is hardly libertine. It confines virtually all sexual activity to heterosexual marriage, and prescribes specific time periods of activity which alternate with periods of abstinence.

The Torah's archetypes are married householders who conduct their spiritual activities within the context of raising a family. *Halakhah* mandates marriage as the normal channel for a life of spiritual growth.

Torah recognizes the sexuality of the male from birth, with the celebration of the *Brit*, the ritual of circumcision. On the eighth day of life, the sexual organ is branded for a spiritual purpose.

Sexual union corresponds to the cosmic unification of male and female within God. The conclusion of the creation of the world was the transition from the masculine, directed-creative side of God into the feminine, receptive-creative part of God. This transition repeats itself in sexual intercourse, particularly on *Shabbat*.

According to Taoism, the life energy of a male is depleted by orgasm and, once used, it cannot be replenished. Therefore, men are urged to avoid orgasm except for procreation in order to increase longevity as well as sexual excitement. In women, on the other hand, orgasm stimulates and increases life. Menstruation, on the other hand, is seen as having a weakening effect. Women are encouraged to be multi-orgasmic and to minimize menses through breathing exercises.[2]

Halakhah holds male orgasm in particular awe. Male masturbation (*Heb. hashhatat zera*, literally, "spilling seed") is regarded as the violation of one of the most important *mizvot*. Erotic thoughts by men are to be avoided, and male homosexual activity is censured. Female masturbation, homosexuality or erotic fantasizing are not similarly condemned.

---

[2]Chai, M., *Taoist Secrets of Love: Cultivating Male Sexual Energy*, New York: Aurora Press, 1984. Chai, M. *Love Through the Tao: Cultivating Male Sexual Energy*. Huntington, New York: Healing Tao Press, 1986

Menstruation and *Tamei*

Menstruation, like male orgasm, is held is great awe. Menstrual blood, paralleling the monthly cycles of the moon, is an essential symbol of the feminine in all nature. Both poetically and actually, the menses springs from the fountain of life. Torah regards the soul's lowest part, the *nefesh*, as residing in blood. Blood is powerful, and menstrual blood especially so. It carries the *nefesh* of a being which never matured. *Halakhah* feels the awe of a the menses so strongly that a man does not touch a woman when she has her period, or even for three days before and seven days afterward.

Torah's attitude toward menstrual blood has been much misunderstood. A woman in her period is not "dirty" and her body is not "unclean." Unfortunately, extremely negative male attitudes toward menstruating women have developed. The intention of *halakhah* was to impress the tremendous awesome feminine power that menstruation symbolizes.

A woman in her menstrual period can be compared to a person who has touched a corpse. Both have been in contact with the mystery of life and death. They are in a state of *tamei*. When a person touches a corpse, they are touching a part of death. They are reminded of their own mortality. The menstruating woman feels the loss of life in the same way. The word *tamei*, best left untranslated, implies this state of being in deepest awareness of life and death. By touching a corpse, menstruating, or giving birth, one becomes *tamei*. In order to reenter a state of *taharah*, its opposite, one must be reborn. This means returning to the spring of life, the primordial water from which all life unfolds.

The *Mikveh*

The *mikveh*, or ritual bath, was originally performed outdoors in a flowing stream, and the ritual can still be done this way. It symbolizes the lifegiving properties of flowing water, and is used by both men and women to celebrate rebirth after contact with death. Converts to Judaism are formally initiated by rebirth in the *mikveh*. Although not a requirement of *halakhah*, some men use the *mikveh* as a means of experiencing an extra measure of spiritual energy on the eve of *Shabbat* and festivals.

Experience 24

Visiting a *Mikveh*

1) Find out if your community has a *mikveh* by calling your local synagogue.

2) To visit it, call ahead. You will probably need an appointment, and someone will probably be delighted to give you a tour. (If there is no *mikveh*, go to the nearest free-flowing river.)

3) If you are inclined to take a dip, the appropriate time for men is on Friday (before sundown) or the day preceding a holiday. The appropriate time for women is seven days after the menstrual period stops. There may be a fee, and if you are not Jewish you may not be allowed. Take along a wash cloth.

4) You enter the water with no clothing, jewelry, makeup, bandages, or anything else that would come between body and water. Enter the water to the chest. Stand in a slight crouch with feet flat on the ground, hands and arms floating. Dunk yourself all the way beneath the water. Then come up and cover your head with the wash cloth you have brought. Recite the blessing:

Barukh ata Adonai	We praise You, Adonai,
Eloheinu melekh haolam	Our God who rules all the universe
Asher kiddshanu	Who sanctifies us with
b'mizvotav vezivanu	Commandments And commands us
Al hat'villah.	About immersion in water

5) After the blessing, remove the wash cloth from your head and dunk yourself two more times.

6) Come out of the water reborn. Luxuriate in the intensity of the mood for as long as you desire.

❖

Reemerging Matriarchy

For the last 4000 years, the Jewish path has been significantly patriarchal. It's archetypes are predominantly male; it's leadership on every level is mostly male; it limits women's civil rights and power in civil law; its images of God are mostly male, despite its indications that God unites male and female together; it makes women's access to God more difficult by limiting involvement with both *aggadah* and *halakah* and it burlesques the positive experience of female energy, power and sexuality into something to be feared.

But on the other hand, the monthly cycle of *taharah* and *tumah* (*tamei*-ness) is more powerful than virtually any other ritual. Women may not need any other ritual. Traditionally, they had no other option, as most of Torah's rituals have excluded women. The current trend toward including women in the full range of Jewish activities is arguably the greatest, most significant change in Judaism in 4000 years.

Male predominance in Jewish ritual has served the important function of requiring men to participate in a spiritual life. Generally speaking, women have a greater spiritual inclination than men. Most men need to do more spiritual work and a bit of coercion just to get to the place where women begin naturally.

This realignment of men's and women's roles in Judaism is an aspect of a universal phenomenon. Throughout the world, in all aspects of culture, women are assuming more active, responsible and creative roles. More women spiritual leaders are emerging, interest in matriarchal images of God is increasing, and traditional attitudes are being questioned. As this trend unfolds, even the most conservative paths will need to make serious accommodations.

Chapter 8

Prophets, Priests and the Paranormal

For the last few hundred years in the West, empirical science and religion have been pitted against each other. Newtonian physics, Cartesian philosophy, and the industrial revolution have conspired to produce a map on which everything in the universe operates by scientifically discoverable principles.

According to this map, mind and matter are two distinct modes. Mind cannot move matter. The human body consists of various chemicals which behave in a perfectly regular, if complex fashion. This map creates a dichotomy between science and religion.

On one side of the dichotomy, the objective, scientific experiment is regarded as a sufficient tool to discover every fact of the universe and its creatures; religion is regarded as ancient superstition. On the other side, religion goes on the defensive. Either it attempts to prove examples of inexplicable phenomenon, or it retreats into an irrational fundamentalism best summed up in the bumper sticker, "God said it, I believe it, that settles it."

Underlying both sides of the dichotomy are the eternal questions: Is there another dimension of reality besides the physical world? Is there a God or gods or emissaries of God who we cannot sense directly, who occasionally interfere and allow something "miraculous" to happen?

Until the last century or two, paranormal or supernatural experiences were an acknowledged part of reality. Every culture had
a designated individual who was the "sacred technician" of the
tribe. Whether called a priest, witch doctor, shaman, medicine
man or woman, or rabbi, he or she played an essential role in
the community. Such a person performed the combined role of
healer, psychologist and physician. His or her job was to facilitate the spiritual growth of the members of the community. Today we are experiencing a revival of this kind of spiritual
leadership, although it is still being ridiculed or ignored by mainstream society.

Supernatural Arts

The sacred technician is trained in the supernatural arts, and
learns a body of knowledge not generally familiar to the rest of
the community. Specifically, there are five primary areas of
knowledge: intuition, healing, prayer, imagination and access
to the unconscious. Each type of knowledge can be honed to such
a degree that its use may appear magical and beyond the understanding of the uninitiated.

Intuition

Intuition is knowledge aquired without apparent cause. Jung
clarified intuition's role as one of the four separate modes of the
mind's function along with ration, emotion, and aesthetic perception. Intuition is an immediate cognition that leaps across
these other three.

An example of intuition might be recognizing a person's unexpressed feeling. Their body language or manner might give
off signals which the intuitive faculty reads. Another example
of intuition is knowing when someone from the past is about
to get in touch, or when a loved one is in danger or ill. Yet
another was voiced by Gauss, the famous mathematician: "I have

had my solutions for a long time, but I do not yet know how I am to arrive at them."[1] Skeptical reductionist attempts to reduce intuition to other categories fail to explain away these rather common experiences.

Intuition implies a unified world view. Each aspect of reality has an interconnection to every other aspect of reality. This ancient metaphysical idea, currently revived by modern physics, explodes the Cartesian-Newtonian model.

Every individual has some intuitive ability, which can be developed by tuning into intuition itself. The sacred technician uses oracles as a means to strengthening intuition. Frequently oversimplified as "fortune telling," an oracle is a device for focusing and increasing intuition. The use of the *I Ching* and Torah's weekly *Sidrah* were described earlier. Another ancient oracle which has found recent renaissance is the Tarot.

The Tarot is a pack of playing cards featuring symbolic drawings on their faces. The twenty-two picture cards called Major Arcana depict twenty-two essential, existential qualities which make up all human experience. Each of these cards reflects awareness of specific archetypes from the collective unconscious.

In consulting the Tarot, one approaches its messages with utmost respect and openness. The reader first deals out the cards into a particular pattern and evaluates the qualities he or she sees the cards indicating. Each card contains just enough ambiguity that hearing this information stimulates the unconscious on an archetypal level. Like other oracles, Tarot understands that every life experience is potentially a means of transformation.

An oracle is a tool for allowing for the experience of the intuition. Repeated use of an oracle strengthens intuition to the point where the uninitiated perceive the sacred technician to be "doing something magic."

---

[1] Deikman, A. *The Observing Self.* Boston: Beacon Press, 1982, p.54

Healing

A second area of knowledge mastered by the sacred technician is healing. This kind of healing combines the skills of internal medicine, psychiatry, massage therapy and faith. Typically,
the holy person has a variety of traditional medicines derived
from animals and herbs. These may physically counteract a disease, or they may stimulate the body's natural ability to heal itself, as in homeopathic medicine. Digitalis and morphine, both
essentials of Western medicine, are ancient natural remedies.

By now, even Western medicine is starting to recognize that
physical disease can be caused by unexpressed emotions. By getting to the root of such repressed feeling, the sacred technician
uses skills akin to modern psychology, perhaps combined with
appropriate rituals to realign the state of mind. The medicine
person often knows how to use touch, massage or body manipulation to cure and balance the body. Touch can massage toxins
from the body, stretch atrophied muscles, stimulate the body's
natural healing ability, open blocked channels of energy, or simply make one feel loved and worthy of being healed.

Prayer

Another tool in the sacred technician's healing arsenal is prayer.
Although many moderns are not convinced of the power of prayer, at least one recent study has indicated how strong the healing power of prayer can be. In 1986, Dr. Randy Byrd, a
cardiologist from the University of California, San Francisco, performed a study in which 393 coronary care unit patients were
divided into two groups.[2] He arranged for prayer groups to
pray for the recovery of the patients in one group, but not the
other. Where there were measurable difference between the two
groups, those prayed upon did consistently better. The subjects

---

[2] Byrd, R. "Positive Therapeutic Effects of Intercessory Prayer in a Coronary Care Unit Population." *The Southern Medical Journal*, Vol. 81. No. 7. p.826ff.

in the first group suffered fewer complications: only three required antibiotics, compared to sixteen in the second group; only six suffered pulmonary edema compared to eighteen in the other group; none required intubation (use of a tube down the throat to permit freer breathing), compared to twelve in the other group.

Byrd recruited a variety of pray-ers to participate. The participants were given the name of a patient, the diagnosis and condition. They were asked to pray each day, for beneficial healing and quick recovery, but no amount of time or way of doing it was specified. Some gathered in groups to pray, but most prayed individually. The patients did not know if they were being prayed upon or not.

The study, which indicates that prayer is a valuable treatment, was accepted for presentation by the prestigious American Heart Association.

Imagination and Astral Projection

Everyone has imagination, the ability to "see" and "hear" things in the mind. In fact, it is the first step to bringing something into existence be it a creative work or a life experience. A very strong imagination can even open the door to astral projection, or "out of body" experience. Medicine people are accredited with the power to leave their bodies. Their imagination becomes so strong that they can imagine themselves flying to another place and seeing it in vivid detail. They are known to appear to people, though they are physically hundreds of miles away.

Similarly, individuals who have had a near-death experience almost always report leaving their bodies and floating upward. They see the room they're in from the vantage point of the ceiling, then proceed to fly upward through a tunnel, toward a great light. Just before reaching the light, they are pulled back down to earth and reconnected to their bodies. Upon recovery, they report seeing things on top of high shelves, hidden from eyeview, which are later confirmed. In addition, they often describe accurately their medical teams struggling to revive them, during the time their eyes were closed. Such accounts are common and testify to the power of the developed imagination to cut beyond the boundaries of time and space.

Access to the Unconscious

The fifth aspect of sacred technology is the ability to help someone access their own unconscious, to learn from it and to use its power. At birth the unconscious contains archetypal material which knows the individual's destiny and which offers guidance and support in all decisions. In addition, the unconscious perceives things differently from the conscious, often far more insightfully. The conscious mind likes to create organizing structures of reality and map out a course while ignoring the unconscious directions. Accessing the unconscious can scramble this false structure to allow the unconscious to emerge.

The unconscious offers up its contents most spontaneously and uncensored through dreams. The content of a significant dream, brought into consciousness and properly understood, is often the first step in a total change of one's life direction.

Although dreams are spontaneous, arising at will and revealing what they choose with almost a mind of their own, there are techniques of dream incubation which appear throughout the world. When a crisis is approaching, a sacred technician can suggest a ritual or meditation which can urge the unconscious to yield an important dream.

How do we know when we are dreaming and when we are in "reality?" The proverbial pinch not withstanding, no one is ever certain. Many people also have the occasional experience of "lucid dreaming," when they dream and within the dream are aware that they are dreaming. By the same token, how do we decide when we look at a picture, which shapes represent which objects in the real world? When pre-technological age people see photographs for the first time, all they discern are random blobs of color.

Access to the unconscious is also possible through a mental "shifting of gears" which is most familiar in the West as hypnosis. Hypnosis is a tool for entering altered states of consciousness through deep mental and physical relaxation. Although different individuals' ability to go into hypnosis vary considerably, most people can diminish pain considerably and modify behavior easily. A minority can even hallucinate in any sensory mode. Hypnotic susceptibility does not seem correlated to any physical, emotional, or mental abilities, other than the will to be hypnotized. Leading someone into a hypnotic state does not require the proverbial swinging watch, but only someone skilled in capturing another's undivided attention. By entering one's unconscious in this way, a shaman can stretch the mind into considering a whole realm of unexplored possibilities.

Gifted sacred technicians are both special and rare, particularly in today's society. A few adepts have chronicled their stories of learning from Native American shamans or Hindu holy persons.

There is much to be gained by learning about a true holy person. Paramahansa Yogananda was a modern individual who became extremely developed in supernatural arts. As an Experience, read his autobiography, *The Autobiography of a Yogi*, suspending your disbelief of any events which appear scientifically impossible.

Dozens of ancient divinatory, intuitive and healing arts have been rediscovered in the last decade. Tarot, astrology, crystals, hypnosis, runes, numerology, healing through touch and acupuncture, and dozens of other arts have begun a slow journey back to Western respectability.

These psychic arts derive their power from the archetypes of the collective unconscious. They have survived for centuries because the human mind demands them. The psyche is constructed in such a way that it knows instinctively that there are types of knowledge that no empirical science can decipher. These arts are programmed so deeply within the workings of the mind that they will never die out.

Today, the supernatural arts are beginning to find defenders even within the scientific community, based on science's own advances. Newtonian physics was long ago abandoned in high school curricula. The existence of subatomic particles, curved space, and the convertibility of matter and energy have replaced the notion that the universe functions simply like balls on a billiard table.

Holographic Model of Reality and the Paranormal

The exile of the paranormal from the Cartesian world was at least logically consistent. However, contemporary freshman physics recognizes that subatomic particles behave like no billiard ball René ever knew.

In recent years, evidence from a variety of academic disciples has converged into rather astounding conclusions. Karl Pribram's research described in *Languages of the Brain*[3] indicates that the brain operates like a hologram. Holography is a method of lensless photography in which the wave field of light scattered by an object is recorded on a plate as an interference pattern. When laser light is directed upon that exposed plate, a three dimensional image appears. If the plate is cut into pieces, any tiny piece of it contains enough information to reconstruct the original whole, although with less detail. Thus each part has the whole encoded within it.

In a similar fashion, modern brain research indicates that stored information when brought to consciousness does not seem to reside in a particular region of the brain, but rather is stored over large areas. Each time the information is accessed, it is gathered together from diverse sources. In instances of brain damage, the network is disrupted but still functioning. These phenomenon

---

[3] Englewood Cliffs, NJ, Prentice Hall, 1971.

indicate that each thought consists of a particular network of cells throughout the brain firing, and that each individual cell knows the structure of that network. Each cell is like a piece of a hologram, encoding all the information, albeit with less detail.

Similarly in sub-atomic physics, David Bohm's[4] work led him to conclude that certain subatomic particles seem to jump in and out of existence frequently, in a rather random fashion but at the same time behaving as though they were following some implicit order. This implicit order is simulateously available to each particle, directing its activity, while it unites all particles together. Thus, the whole physical universe resembles a megahologram, with each part belonging to the whole and encoding the whole within it.

From this follows the "holographic paradigm:" the brain is a hologram perceiving and participating in a holographic universe. In the explicit, manifest realm of time and space, things and events are separate and distinct from one another. Beneath the surface is the implicate or frequency realm where all things and events are spacelessly, timelessly, intrinsically one and undivided.[5] Logically either the same hand drew them both or else this is an amazing accident which just happens to also confirm the ancient alchemical intuition, "As above, so below."

In a world governed by such "illogical" physical science, paranormal events no longer contradict the seamless, regular functioning of the universe that everyone expects.

Synchronicity

Jung once devised experiments correlating predictions made by astrological forecasts about who would marry whom, with the facts of who actually did get married. Jung himself was astonished to discover the accuracy of the predictions. They beat the odds

---

[4] *Quantum Theory and Beyond*, Cambridge University 1971.
[5] *The Holographic Paradigm*, K. Wilber, ed. New Science Library, Boulder, CO, 1982.

of random chance by an extraordinary percent. Unable to explain these results by any scientific theory, he coined the term "synchronicity"—"meaningful coincidence." Synchronicity supports a universe where every event is interwoven.

Experience 25

Acknowledging Synchronicity

1) Think back over some of the major decisions you've made in your life, choices involved where to live, what to study, what career to pursue, who to marry, etc.

2) In recalling these choices, look for any events which occurred at the time which influenced your decision.

3) Ask yourself if this might be evidence of guidance from another plane upon your life.

❖

Prophets of the Paranormal and Sages of the Supernatural

Judaism has always had a very strong supernatural component. From its origins until the nineteenth century, Judaism has celebrated the paranormal. But over the last 150 years, supernaturalism has gradually been excised from the religion. With the advent of the Age of Science, the quest for the experience of God began to take a back seat to technology. In order to survive in modern times, Judaism put on a straighter face.

The Torah does warn about delving into some facets of paranormal experience. It demands: "Let no one be found among you who...is an auger, a soothsayer, a diviner, a sorcerer. One who casts spells or who consults ghost or familiar spirits, or who enquires of the dead. For anyone who does such things is abhorrent to *YHVH*." (DEUTERONOMY 18 10-12). Throughout the ages, however, these words have been understood in various ways. Some of our greatest rabbis have said that it forbids the practice of astrology, and yet others among our greatest teachers have been famous for their abilities as astrologers. This passage would seem to forbid any type of séance. Yet the Talmud is full of stories of great rabbis who die and return to visit their students and teach them further important lessons. Others among our greatest teachers have had spirit guides who appeared to direct their work or were reputed to cast spells over those who disobeyed them.

Every important Jewish hero has been a sacred technician of extraordinary supernatural powers. However, most modern students of Judaism "de-mythologize" the supernatural feats of Talmudic wonderworkers, medieval saints, and Hasidic Rebbes as folklore.

The Torah assumes the reality of these powers, and it attributes some of them to every one of its major characters. Abraham had the intuitive power to know about his descendants' enslavement in Egypt (GENESIS 15:13). His wife Sarah received healing which permitted her to become pregnant long after menopause, and Abraham's intuition brought him foreknowledge of this event (GENESIS 17:19). He also knew about the forthcoming disasters to the cities of Sodom and Gomorah, and applied his considerable powers of prayer to try and avert them (GENESIS 18:24f).

When Abraham sent a servant to look for a wife for Isaac, an oracle was employed which selected Rebecca (GENESIS 24:10f). Later, when Rebecca had a difficult pregnancy, she consulted an oracle which told her that the twins growing within her were already engaged in a lifelong struggle for dominance over each other (GENESIS 25:21).

When Rebecca's son Jacob matured, his imagination was so

strong that he experienced God directly in his dreams (GENESIS
28:12f) and he trusted that experience to guide the direction of
his life. His son, Joseph, inherited his father's talent for understanding dreams. As a youth, Joseph's dreams prefigured his entire life (GENESIS 37:5f). Later, his ability to interpret dreams freed
him from prison (GENESIS 40:4) and facilitated his becoming the
second most powerful person in the world (GENESIS 41:1f).

Moses demonstrated the greatest knowledge of the paranormal. His facility with imagination and intuition gave him the
power to make others believe his staff could become a serpent
(EXODUS 7:8). An entire nation witnessed his power to inflict ten
unpleasant plagues upon them (EXODUS 7:20ff). He knew enough
about tides that he saved the Israelites while the Egyptian army
drowned (EXODUS 14:15f). During forty years in the desert he always found food and water for thousands of people. His prayers
healed his sister's leprosy (NUMBERS 12:10f). He survived challenge
to his leadership by commanding the earth to open and swallow
up his opponents (NUMBERS 16:28f). He directed the creation of
the Urim and Tummim, a dice-like oracle which the priests continued to use for centuries (EXODUS 28:30; I SAMUELS 14:41).

Judaism's trust in the paranormal was by no means confined
to the Torah. The prophets who followed the Torah for the next
800 years were similarly adept. Under Joshua's leadership, the
conquest of the Land of Israel was facilitated by supernatural
events, such as the drying up of the river Jordan (JOSHUA 3:15f)
and the miraculous destruction of Jericho (JOSHUA 6:11f).

During the next period of the "Judges," visions of angels instructed the nation in the meaning of their history (JUDGES 2:1)
and chose their leaders for them (JUDGES 6:11; 13:2). During the
time of Samuel's leadership, the Ark of God was captured by
the Philistines and brought into their temple, where it destroyed
the statue of their god (I SAMUELS 5:2). Samuel's intuition guided him to select Saul as Israel's first king (I SAMUELS 9:15) and to
predict signs which would later verify this choice (I SAMUELS 10:3f).
Samuel's own experience of God also confirmed his choice

(I SAMUELS 10:9f). During Saul's reign, Saul consults a medium to conjure Samuel's spirit to tell him the outcome of a forthcoming battle. Samuel appears, angry at having been disturbed from his sleep, and tells Saul that he will lose (I SAMUELS 28:8).

When David succeeded Saul as king, he consulted the prophetic oracle when he wanted to build a Temple to God, but his request was denied (II SAMUELS 7:1f). His son, Solomon, also invoked *YHVH's* word before fulfilling his father's wish and building the Temple (II SAMUELS 810f).

The kings and leaders who followed had numerous encounters with highly intuitive prophets, who often predicted the future. The preeminent figures at this time were Elijah and Elisha. Elijah healed a child near death (I KINGS 17:17), overpowered the non-Israelite prophets (I KINGS 18:25ff), received oracles about whom to make king and which kings would be deposed (I KINGS 19:15 and 21:20), and brought down fire from heaven which killed fifty men (II KINGS 1:10).When Elijah was about to die, a flaming chariot descended from heaven to carry him away (II KINGS 2:6f).

Elijah's successor, Elisha, turned salt water into fresh (II KINGS 2:19), conjured bears to mangle children who were harrassing him (II KINGS 2:23), filled dozens of jugs of oil from one jugful (II KINGS 4:5), caused an old woman to become pregnant (II KINGS 4:16), and later revived her child from death (II KINGS 4:29f). He fed hundreds of hungry people with a few loaves of bread (II KINGS 5:42), healed lepers (II KINGS 5:13), made an axe float on water (II KINGS 6:5), made other people have visions (II KINGS 6:17f), predicted an end to the siege of Samaria (II KINGS 7:1), and predicted monarchic succession (II KINGS 8:7f).

The three great "writing prophets" who followed, Isaiah, Jeremiah and Ezekiel, facilitated far fewer miraculous events, but their intuitions were extremely strong. They frequently perceived political events before they happened. Their descriptions of God were so vivid that they established the predominant patterns of describing the experience of God ever since. Isaiah's portrait of God's throne (ISAIAH 1) and Ezekiel's elaborate description of

God's chariot (EZEKIEL 1) have fueled the imagination of spiritual teachers and seekers for 2500 years. Jeremiah learned that his
mission was ordained for him before he was even conceived
(JEREMIAH 1), thus establishing a Jewish intimation of reincarnation. Because their strong intuitions placed them at odds with
the rulers of their time, these three prophets were ostracized from
society.

The Talmud and Midrash literature contain literally thousands
of stories which attribute different powers to the rabbis of that
age. These tales assumed that the great rabbis had the power
to both heal and harm, sometimes simply with words. Even a
look from a powerful rabbi was enough to affect one's personality, or even cause death. The power, though acquired through
the Torah, was not always a blessing, as the tale of Naḥum of
Gamzo demonstrates:

> Naḥum was blind in both eyes, had stumps for hands, was crippled
> in both legs, and his entire body was inflicted with sores. When his
> disciples inquired as to his dilemma, he revealed that he had imposed
> these travails upon himself! Once, while journeying on the road with
> three asses laden with food, drink and delicacies, he'd been approached
> by a stranger asking for something to eat. Naḥum replied that he wanted
> first to dismount from his ass. After doing so, he turned to find the
> man dead. He realized his lack of compassion — for even one moment —
> had caused the tragedy. In penalty for his lapse, he inflicted his condi-
> tion upon himself. (B. TA'ANIT 21A)

In addition, the Talmud contains an elaborate manual on
dream interpretation (B. BERAKHOT 55A f) and proscribes rituals
to observe on the morning following disturbing dreams. This
ritual can still be found in an occasional unexpurgated prayerbook. In this ritual, the dreamer reports the dream to his or her
prayergroup, who responds with blessings and assurances that
the dream is only for one's benefit, not harm.

Sefer Yeẓirah, Tarot and Astrology

The sacred technician's use of oracles to sharpen intuition finds a Judaic manifestation in the *Sefer Yeẓirah*, "Book of Forma-tion," especially when it is considered in its congruence to Tarot and astrology. An early (at least 1500 years old) much beloved Jewish spiritual text, the *Sefer Yeẓirah* presents a brief summary of metaphysics in an oracular framework.

Sefer Yeẓirah subdivides all experience into thirty-two differ-ent categories which correspond to the ten numerals and the twenty-two letters of the Hebrew alphabet. The ten numerals refer to the ten *sephirot*. *Sefer Yeẓirah* divides the twenty-two letters into the three primal "mother letters," from which evolve the seven "double" letters, from which unfold the twelve "sim-ple" letters. The mother letters represent the elements, air, fire and water. The double letters represent the days of the week, the orifices of the body, and the seven traditional planets of as-trology. The simple letters represent the signs of the zodiac, the months of the year, organs of the body and diagonal directions.

The Tarot, like astrology, is one of the most enduring Western oracles. At least 600 years old, it is the direct ancestor of modern playing cards. Like astrology, Tarot is often wrongly perceived in the West as "fortune telling," somehow knowing the future through unlikely portents. In fact, these oracles are the early precursors to psychotherapy or Jungian analytical psychology.

In a Tarot reading, cards are dealt in a pattern which initiates a process of reflection, meditation and free-association between the Reader and the Inquirer about the meaning of the images which appear. When interpreting an astrological chart, a simi-lar process takes place.

The Tarot's twenty-two cards of the Major Arcana represent stages on life's journey. The process begins with the Fool, the first card, who slings his pack over his back and sets off to ex-plore any adventure imaginable from selling securities to skydiv-ing. The process concludes with the World, the last card, where everything has evolved into a higher new harmony. In between the other twenty cards represent the mythic process of transform-ation.

The twenty-two cards of the Major Arcana correspond to twenty-two astrological signs—the twelve signs of the zodiac, the seven traditional astrologic "planets" (Mercury, Venus, moon, sun, Mars, Jupiter, Saturn), and the three more recently discovered distant planets (Uranus, Neptune, Pluto). Astrology, like other oracles, uses archetypal symbols to understand the process unfolding, rather than predict.

Each Tarot card/Hebrew letter/astrological body suggest similar qualities. The first card, the Fool, is the first letter Aleph and the planet Uranus. The Fool begins the process. Aleph has no consonantal sound but only vocalizes the vowel conjoined to it. As the first letter, it has a particular magical quality and it is the element air. It is the first sound God speaks at Sinai, barely audible but crashing like thunder. Uranus, because it was the first planet discovered (in 1784) by technologic advances over the naked eye, represents revolutionary change. Its appearance indicates the unconventional and the unusual. It is regarded as the planet of both good and bad surprises and therefore it is a teacher.

The second card, the magician, is the sacred technician who intrudes upon the Fool. He plays tricks to help us see beyond the narrow horizons of our experience. The second letter *Bet* is the first letter of the creation of the world which sets the boundary between human and infinite. Shaped like a backwards "C" on an elongated base," *Bet* has three closed sides and one open side, indicating the boundaries between experience that is manifest and experience that is hidden. *Bet* and the Magician correspond to Mercury, the Trickster, who upsets our plans with his own. Mercury leads us into our worst times of suffering, but stays with us offering guidance through the process.

The third card, the High Priestess or the Papess is pure *yin* energy, the primordial matriarch. Her planet is the moon, whose waxing and waning is a sign of the eternal feminine. The third letter, Gimel, means "camel," but also suggests "*gomayl*," the aspect of God as Renewing and Preserving Force. (See following Chart

#	Name	Letter	Type and Attributes per Sefer Yezirah	Tarot Card	Astrologic Sign
0	Aleph	א	3: spirit, air, body, abundance	Fool	Uranus
1	Bet	ב	7: life, Sunday, right eye	Magician	Mercury
2	Gimel	ג	7: health, Monday, left eye	Papesse	Moon
3	Dalet	ד	7: wisdom, Tuesday, right ear	Empress	Venus
4	Hay	ה	12: sight, *Nisan*, right hand	Emperor	Aries
5	Vav	ו	12: hearing, *Iyar* left hand	Pope	Taurus
6	Zayin	ז	12: smell, *Sivan*, right foot	Lover	Gemini
7	Het	ח	12: speech, *Tamuz*, left foot	Chariot	Cancer
8	Tet	ט	12: eating, *Av*, right kidney	Justice	Leo
9	Yud	י	12: coition, *Elul*, left kidney	Hermit	Virgo
10	Kaf	כ	7: wealth, Wednesday, left ear	Wheel of Fortune	Jupiter
11	Lamed	ל	12: work, *Tishre*, liver	Force	Libra
12	Mem	מ	3: water, earth, cold, abdomen	Hanged Man	Neptune
13	Nun	נ	12: walking, *Marhesvan*, spleen	Death	Scorpio
14	Samah	ס	12: anger, *Kislev*, gallbladder	Temperance	Sagittarius
15	Ayin	ע	12: laughing, *Tevet*, colon	Devil	Capricorn
16	Pay	פ	7: beauty, Thursday, right nostril	Tower of God/ Destruction	Mars
17	Zadee	צ	12: thought, *Shevat*, stomach	Star	Aquarius
18	Koof	ק	12: sleep, *Adar*, small intestine	Moon	Pices
19	Resh	ר	7: fruitfulness, Friday, left nostril	Sun	Sun
20	Shin	ש	3: heaven, heat, head	Judgement	Pluto
21	Tav	ת	7: dominion, Shabbat, mouth	World	Saturn

for the congruences of all twenty-two letters/signs/cards.)

1500 years before the most distant planets were discovered, *Sefer Yeẓirah* reserved places for them to correspond to the three remaining letters and the Tarot's structure anticipated them. In this technological age, this synchronicity reinforces the intuitive attraction of these ancient oracles.

The most commen Tarot deck, the Rider-Waite design, includes the word "Tora" on two occasions. The Rider-Waite is a rather stylized 19th-Century deck incorporating many symbols not found in earlier decks. However, the extreme popularity of this deck indicates the depth of archetypal connections which it facilitates. The High Priestess card holds a scroll which says, "Tora," indicating the dynamic process of Torah, rather than "the Torah." The Wheel of Fortune, which represents the transitory nature of everything, depicts a wheel whose spinning endlessly spells out *YHVH*, the most sacred name of God, and endlessly permutes into "Tora" and "Taro."

In each oracle, however, these same twenty-two archetypal categories sort and focus intuitive material for the sacred technician's use. The *Sefer Yeẓirah* bridges Torah to Tarot, as well as to astrology.

Book of *Zohar*

Next to the Bible and the Talmud, the Jewish book which has been most revered through the ages is the *Zohar*, or the *Book of Splendor*. This thirteenth century commentary on the Torah is an explication of the metaphysics of the *sephirot*. Its basic premise is that everything in the universe is part of God and that nothing is static. There is a constant cosmic interplay of the *sephirot*, the Divine Aspects which regulate everything that occurs both in the universe and in the individual human.

The *Zohar* is a virtual textbook of the supernatural. Concerning dreams, it teaches:

When people are lying in their beds asleep, the soul leaves them....then the Holy Blessed One reveals to the soul...things that are destined to come about in the world, or things that correspond to the mind's reflections, so that the dreamer will respond to the warning. Nothing is revealed while the person is under the spell of the body. Rather, an angel tells the soul and the soul tells the person. (ZOHAR I:183A-B).

The *Zohar* notes that intuition is an essential element in spiritual growth:

Come and see: Certain colors can be seen and certain colors cannot. Both are the high mystery of faith. No one was pure enough to see the colors that can be seen until the Patriarchs came and mastered them. But no human being except Moses has mastered the colors above that are invisible. Who is enlightened? The wise one who contemplates the words that human beings cannot mouth that come from deep within. (ZOHAR II:23A-B).

Moses Maimonides

Moses Maimonides (1135-1204) is generally regarded as the greatest Jewish teacher of the Middle Ages. His *Guide to the Perplexed* is extreme in its attempt to provide scientific and non-supernatural understanding of the miraculous events of the Bible and Talmud. Maimonides argued that the Torah used language and metaphor to hide a scientific understanding of the world behind fanciful images.

However, the *Guide's* last chapter indicates that Maimonides' rationalism had limits of its own. The chapter is a lesson on attaining the gift of prophecy, which Maimonides hinted he had already acquired or was soon to reach.

The providence of God...is constantly watching over those who have obtained this prophesy, which is permitted to everyone who makes efforts ...to obtain it. If a man's thought is free from distraction, if he apprehends God... in the right way and rejoices in what he apprehends, that individual can never be afflicted with evil of any kind. For he is with God and God is with him (*Guide to the Perplexed* 3:51).

Thus, the extreme skeptic of the supernatural hoped to achieve paranormal experience as the end product of his rationalism.

Yosef Karo

Another important teacher is Yosef Karo (1488-1575), who wrote two of the greatest treatises on *halakhah*: the *Bet Yosef* and the *Shulḥan Arukh*. The latter is the codification of the *halakhah* whose authority has been unquestioned among observant Jews up to the present day. Next to the Bible and the Talmud, it is Judaism's most studied and honored book.

Yosef Karo was also an adept in the sacred arts. He was a member of the circle of initiates of Rabbi Isaac Luria of Safed, Israel, which included many of the greatest Jewish spiritual teachers of all time. Karo received regular visitations from a disembodied spirit, or "*maggid*" which spoke through Karo. It identified itself as "*Mishnah*" (the core of the oral Torah) or "*Shekhinah*." Today, this would be called channeling. The *maggid* instructed Karo on methods of attaining the experience of God, secrets of reincarnation, meditations, esoteric understanding of the Torah, and even subtle points of *halakhah*.

Hasidism

Hasidism was a Jewish movement of spiritual renewal which spread through Eastern European Jewry in the eighteenth century. Its early leaders were preachers and rabbis who attached themselves to the Baal Shem Tov (d. 1760), a rabbi and wonderworker whose teachings became the focus of the movement. Hasidism was filled with an appreciation for the paranormal, as thousands of miraculous events are attributed to the Baal Shem Tov and the masters who followed him. Indeed, much of Hasidic literature consists of "tales" which are reports of the masters' "sacred skills." The Jews we see dressed in long black coats, bushy fur hats, and long side curls are among the remnants of the Hasidic movement which still exists.

Gaon Of Vilna

The leading opponent of the early phase of the Hasidic movement was Elijah ben Solomon Zalman of Vilna (1720-97), also known as the Gaon (Exalted Sage) of Vilna. Because of his fierce opposition, he is often wrongly portrayed as an unbending rationalist. However, he was also a gifted sacred technician who studied and wrote of the esoteric secrets of Torah. Like Karo, he treasured the teachings of Isaac Luria. He meditated, and he too was visited by a *maggid*.

Exorcism

Another aspect of paranormal experience, exorcism, has also been conspicuous in the Jewish past. There are ancient rituals for exorcism. A *dibbuk* ("one that clings") is the soul of someone who died having suffered a serious injustice. The unfortunate, disembodied soul then takes over the body of another until justice can be done. Usually the *dibbuk* acts maliciously and causes harm to his or her host body. The thread connecting reports of *dibbuks* through the centuries goes back 2000 years. Only exorcism can free the one possessed of the *dibbuk*. Exorcism is a ritual in which the sacred technician plunges into the unconscious of the possessed to release the unconscious material.

A benign cousin of the *dibbuk* is the *ibbur* ("impregnation"), which enters into another for the specific purpose of performing certain acts or *mizvot*. This provides the soul of a departed saint a final opportunity to complete a life of perfect obedience to Torah, when one commandant remained unfulfilled.

A few great rabbis have had such tremendous paranormal power attributed to them that they were able to create a human-like creature. A *golem* ("body without form") is a Frankenstein-type being, a human created by a human. The most famous *golem* known belonged to Rabbi Judah Loew of Prague (d.1609), but the earliest reported *golem* belonged to the Talmudic sage, Rava (B. SANHEDRIN 65B).

Rabbi Judah created his *golem* by reciting the correct pronunciation of the tetragrammaton in his ear. He hoped that the *golem* would protect the Jews of Prague but the *golem* turned on those it was supposed to protect and had to be destroyed.

Paranormal Reentry

Science has discovered what the spiritual traditions have always known: the world is not as simple as it seems. The liberal religion that came with the technological age excised the supernatural as it bleached out the experience of God. The paranormal is such an intrinsic part of the Jewish path, however, that historic continuity would demand a reexamination, even if experience of the archetypes did not keep raising its troublesome head.

Paranormal events happen rarely enough that many people find it easy to ignore their existence. However, when they do occur, they have a tendancy to happen with certain dramatic flair. If even one supernatural event occurs, just once, then the reality of different levels of experience becomes certain. Intuition, imagination, healing, prayer, and entry into another's consciousness are subtle, yet powerful human skills which deserve to be restored to their lost positions of honor.

Chapter 9

Meditation

The Royal Road to the Consciousness of God

Prayer, dietary regulations, sacrifices, celebrations, song, dance and other spiritual disciplines can be found in almost every culture, in every age. In the West, the most basic religious activity is prayer. However, in many other cultures, and in all Eastern religions, the preeminent spiritual activity is meditation.

If prayer is "talking to God," meditation is "listening." We in the West are better at talking than at listening. Western acquaintance with the meditational traditions of the East were virtually unknown until the 1960's, when the Beatles became involved with the Guru Maharishi Mahesh Yogi. Since then, the West's interest in Eastern spirituality has grown steadily. Words like karma and dharma no longer need to be translated every time they appear.

At the same time, this trend has triggered increased curiosity in the West about its own hidden analogs to Eastern spirituality. Churches and synagogues now offer workshops in meditative practices of their own traditions. Many people have an easier time with the idea of meditation than of prayer. To many, prayer seems like asking a Transcendent God to intervene on one's behalf. Meditation is looking inside to contact the Divine within. Meditation requires no God-Who-Is-Beyond to comprehend.

Yet, actually practicing meditation is difficult for most Westerners. People often worry about the reasons to meditate or are concerned about doing it "the right way." For one reason or another, they never quite get around to doing it.

Imagine talking to someone in a room where the air conditioning is on, but you are not aware of its being on, until it clicks off. Suddenly, you realize how quiet it is—and how loudly you were talking before. Two different sound processes were happening at the same time, but you were only aware of your conversation. Similarly, our minds have more than one thing happening at one time, but we are only aware of our conscious, rational mind. Meditation is turning off that program and listening for others.

Meditation is a process of entering into an alternative state of consciousness. We spend most of our waking time in the "common consensus state of consciousness" (CCSC). This is the mental state in which we do most of our daily activities, and where things unfold according to predictable scientific causality.

The most familiar alternative state of consciousness is the dream state. In dreams, things happen without identifiable causality. People and objects appear and disappear as if by magic. There are other alternative states which meditation can bring about, different from CCSC, though usually more reasonable than the dream state. Reaching these states does not come automatically on the first meditative experience, but they can be facilitated by practice.

Practicing

Meditation doesn't require twisting oneself into a lotus position, becoming a vegetarian, donning a loincloth, or anything else out of the ordinary.

Meditation begins by simply focusing the mind on one particular thing: a thought, an image, a candle, a word, a movement, breathing, or even on nothingness. By focusing on one thing, all other day-to-day thoughts and activities are "put on the shelf."

Meditation begins by choosing one particular thing to focus upon. It proceeds by keeping the mind focused on that thing for a period of time. Five minutes is acceptable for a beginner. A goal of reaching twenty minutes is ambitious.

Five minutes, you may discover, is quite a long time. After a minute or so, the mind wanders...you wonder what you will do when you finish meditating...then you remember you are supposed to be meditating and return to your center of focus. A moment or so later, you can't remember if you turned off the iron or experience some other random thought about your everyday life...and start to worry...then remember you are supposed to be meditating. Soon, you feel that crick in the back of your neck...you shift your position, then return your focus. You focus for a bit, then remember that the day after tomorrow is your sister's birthday and you'd better remember to call her....and on and on it goes.

On the first several tries at meditating, it's difficult to keep the mind focused on one thing. Every time it wanders, you must simply put the thought that interrupts your focus "on a shelf" and return to your point of focus. When beginning, you may find it helpful to keep a pad and pen nearby to write down those intrusive thoughts, then return to your meditating.

In the beginning, you may find yourself trying hard to "do it right," or thinking you're "no good at it." Relax. There is no right or wrong, and there are no shortcuts. The process must unfold in its proper way. You wouldn't expect to learn a foreign language in one or two short, easy lessons. Learning to meditate is a skill that must develop in the same way. The important thing is to watch the process.

Experience 26

Candle Meditation

1) Choose a comfortable seat in a dark room where you won't be disturbed.

2) Light a candle, place it a couple feet in front of you. If you have a timer, set it for five minutes.

3) Focus your eyes and your attention on the candle. If your mind wanders, put the interruption aside and refocus your attention on the candle.

4) Repeat the practice as often as you like, but resolve to do it at least once a day for a week.

5) If you are inclined, experiment with lengthening your meditation periods gradually, adding a minute or two every few days, until you can meditate for twenty minutes.

❖

After repeated meditation, the mind begins to slow down. The interruptions occur at longer intervals. As you begin watching the endless parade of thoughts, you realize how active, busy and untamed the mind is. Imagine you are sitting at the bank of a river. Every once in a while something comes floating down the river, from a boatful of people to a handful of trash. It floats into your view, then out again. When you begin meditating, the river is a raging white-water after a cloudburst has dumped all sorts of flotsam upstream. After a while, the river calms down. You simply observe each object as it enters, then departs.

After a while at this practice, interesting things begin to happen. You may find that you are more relaxed and happier, or that you have more energy and are more creative. You may be able to better express your emotions, or perceive sensory images.

Your dreams may become more vivid and easier to remember. Your intuition may become clearer and more accurate. Meditation is not a panacea for all of life's problems, but it is a powerful tool for spiritual growth.

Meditation is a spiritual discipline. Its goal is to loosen the attachments which blind us from our true purpose on this earth. It's purpose is to elevate our energies from the lower *chakras/ sephirot* to the higher centers and to unleash the energy of the *neshamah*, the Higher Self. The ultimate goal of meditating is to facilitate the experience of God.

Where to Focus

The path that your journey will take is determined in part by what you have focused upon, which can be anything. Every spiritual tradition recommends certain words, phrases, objects, pictures or sensory experiences. Such choices are not made lightly, for whatever is meditated upon will be reinforced in both your consciousness and unconsciousness. If you meditate on something mundane, the experience will likely be banal.

Therefore, it is advisable that you choose an object that will help facilitate the experience of God. A candle is an effective object for centering. The strong contrast between the flame and the dark room helps the eyes to lock into the light and remain there without effort, almost hypnotically. Furthermore, light is a symbol of God. It is an almost totally nonmaterial substance. In the Torah's account, God's calling light into being begins the creation of the world.

There are five major types of awareness-focusing devices found throughout the world. Three of them are best known by their sanskrit names: mantra, mandala and hathayoga. The fourth is "visualization." The fifth is "nothingness."

Mantra

A mantra is a word, name of God, or spiritual phrase that is repeated over and over again. The constant repetition of a sound with spiritual significance not only focuses consciousness, but also connects the speaker with the sacred. The most widely used mantra in India is *om*, pronounced AH-OWM. The endlessly repeated, long, basso chanting of AH-OWM on the exhalation, followed by the silence of inhalation, assumes an entire metaphysics in a single syllable.

In Tibet, the most popular mantra is *OM mani padme him* (pronounced AHOWM-MAH-NAY PAHD-MAY HOOM). It means "All-that-there-is, is a precious jewel in the lotus flower which blooms in my heart." In Nepal, there are rocks twenty feet long and ten feet high with *OM mani padme hum* written thousands of times in tiny letters. There are prayer wheels at temples with the mantra written in them millions of times.

In Islam, the practice known as *zikr* is a meditation in which the names of God are continually repeated. First mentioned in the Koran and elaborated through the Sufi tradition, in *zikr* the recitation of the names of God are accompanied with carefully controlled movements and breathing.

Zen Buddhism has developed a complete science of mantra-like *koans*. The best known *koans* contain within themselves an apparent paradox, such as the proverbial, "What is the sound of one hand clapping?" The paradox teaches us that it is only our own dualistic thinking that divides the world into right and wrong, good and bad, friend and enemy. By penetrating into the *koan*, the apparent dualism is transcended. Other *koans* emphasize expanding awareness of life, remaining free of attachments to things, and living in harmonic accord with nature.

Mandala

A mandala is a picture that consists of a series of concentric geometric figures, particularly squares and circles. When meditated upon, it directs the viewer to its center, and becomes engraved in the consciousness.

The great stained glass Rose window of the Cathedral of Chartres is a mandala, as are the Star (or Shield) of David, the layout of the obelisks at Stonehenge, the Mayan stone calendar, Navajo sand paintings, the Christian cross, the lotus flower, a snowflake, and the Earth itself.

The mandala depicts the psyche of the individual, the entire universe and the Oneness of God. In meditating on the mandala, we are reminded that the microcosm (the individual) and the macrocosm (the universe) are analogous.

Jung had his analysands draw mandalas to represent the different stages of their analysis. The mandala thus became a therapeutic tool: in projecting his or her own mental state upon the mandala's grid, the analysand separated from his or her own mind, and was liberated from that particular mental state.

Movement

Although most meditation is done while sitting still, the third major type of focusing involves movement, dance, awareness of the body, and physical exercise. The flow of energy in the body, its stance, position and movement can all be meditation. Hathayoga, perhaps the best known meditation of movement, consists of a set of postures, each of which embodies a specific attitude and relation to the universe. Just as bowing in prayer facilitates prayer, and putting up your fists facilitates aggression or self-defense, so each of the hathayoga postures facilitates opening the body's energy to specific experiences.

T'ai chi, like other Oriental martial arts, is a series of carefully choreographed dance-like movements which originated as a meditative practice and martial art. Each movement is danced with total concentration, until the dancer becomes completely identified with the experience and loses the sense of personal self.

Sufi dancing is a moving meditation from the Islamic tradition, in which one simultaneously walks, breathes with conscious body control, and chants a catalog of different names of God.

Visualization

The goal of directed visualization is to bring into consciousness the image upon which one is meditating. Unlike ordinary fantasies or daydreams, however, in spiritual visualization the mind focuses on a holy image. We tap into the spiritual qualities within ourselves that are represented by the image. In order to imagine Buddha, sitting serenely and all-knowing beneath the Bodhi tree, we must summon forth our own intuitive knowledge of serenity and enlightenment. Repeated visualization strengthens that knowledge and eventually brings it in to our normal consciousness.

According to Tantric tradition, through meditation on an image of a god, one enters into the cosmic plane which that god rules, and its sacred force becomes manifest within the meditator. Tantric texts provide minute descriptions of the gods to be visualized, complete with often horrible, grotesque details. In one source, the goddess Durga wears wreathes of skulls around her neck, thousands of dead hands on her hips, and two infant corpses for earrings.[1] Visually creating her is the first step to deflating the horror she provokes.

In another type of tantric visualization, one visualizes particular lotus flowers upon the *chakras* of the body. Each *chakra* is ruled by a particular divinity who is imagined to reside there.

Nothingness

When you meditate on nothingness, you clear your mind of everything. You focus your awareness on the empty space in front

---

[1]Eliade, M. *Yoga, Immortality and Resurrection*. Princeton: Princeton University Press, 1958, p. 208.

of your eyes, like a blank black board. While you know that this space is "something," you are actually focused on "nothing." This is the essential paradox of meditating on nothingness. The moment nothingness enters your consciousness, it becomes something.

Filling ones mind with nothingness, clears the mind of all perception. With the senses turned off, the mind is open to the most subtle, spiritual influences that come from within and without. In most traditions, meditating on nothingness is considered an advanced technique.

A Zen-Buddhist type of meditation on nothingness is called *Shikantaza*, "nothing but sitting." Zen's usual focusing devices, counting the breath or contemplating a *koan*, are absent. In this practice, the mind must be unhurried and firmly composed "like Mt. Fuji," yet alert and ready "like a taut bow-string."

Listening to God

Meditation does not appear to be the most important spiritual activity in Judaism. Interacting with *aggadah* and *halakhah*, davening, celebration of *Shabbat* and festivals, and adherence to *kashrut* and *taharah* are the predominant elements facilitating the experience of God. However, the practice of meditation does exist in the Jewish tradition, and is called *Hitbodedut* (withdrawing inward) or *Deveikut* (clinging to God).

In addition, davening has a meditational component. When davening is "talking to God" it is prayer; when it is "listening" it becomes meditation.

The daily service can be understood as a mantra. Most mantras are short and recited for a number of minutes. Davening the service is reciting a many paged mantra one time. Each time you daven the mantra/service, a different experience unfolds. The words take on new meaning as you express them according to your needs and emotions at that moment.

One central part of the service, the *Shema* and her blessings is itself three short meditations on the "Oneness of God," "the workings of karma," and "the Torah in your life." By reading each paragraph, the mind focuses on each of these ideas. The first blessing before the *Shema* is a meditation on "God created the world," the second is "God loves Israel," and then the *Shema* itself followed by the blessing "Release from Egypt" afterward. As you daven the *Shema* and her blessings, you go through this series of meditations. Twice-daily meditation on the *Shema* and her blessings is one of the most important of the Torah's 613 *mizvot* which make up the Way of *Halakhah*.

Meditation in Biblical and Post-Biblical Judaism

The Hebrew Bible records many visionary experiences, but only hints at the meditational practices which helped facilitate them. In post-Biblical times, however, we have far more extensive accounts of meditation. Mantra meditation has been a part of Jewish practice for nearly 2000 years. *The Heikhalot Rabbati*, "Tremendous Palaces," is one of the most ancient surviving Jewish texts describing the experience of God. It describes visions that can be experienced as one ascends through a variety of chambers and palaces, until ultimately arriving at the vision of God sitting upon a celestial throne. In order to achieve this vision, one must repeat 112 times a particular name of God which is composed of twelve tongue-twisting words.

Several of the great spiritual teachers of the Sixteenth century community of Safed, Israel, used verses from the Bible or the *Mishnah* as mantras. Moshe Cordevero (1522-1570) developed a complex technique of using Bible verses as mantras. Yosef Karo adapted Cordevero's techniques, but used verses from the *Mishnah* as his mantra.

One of the great masters of the Hasidic movement, Naḥman of Bratslav (1772-1811), advised his followers that:

> Meditation is the highest path of all. One must therefore set aside

an hour or more each day to meditate by himself in a room or in the field. [2]

Naḥman also recommended the use of the name of God, *Rebono Shel Olam,* "Master of the Universe," as a general purpose mantra that would aid anyone in their spiritual quest.

Mantra and the Names of God

The Safed circle produced the most developed system of mantra meditation in Jewish tradition, meditation on a name of God. A name of God upon which one meditates is called a *yiḥud,* "unification." The unpronounceable fourletter name of God, *YHVH* is often used as a mantra. The letters of this name are frequently combined with letters from other names of God to create words which appear to be nonsense, but are in fact words of great power. Each name of God is connected to one of the *sephirot,* and meditation upon that name brings one into direct contact with that *sephirah.*

Experience 27

Meditation on the Names of God

1) Sit comfortably where you won't be disturbed. Breath deeply until you are relaxed.

2) Center your attention on the name *YHVH,* or the Hebrew, יהוה . Be aware that this name is connected with the *sephirah ḥokhmah,* which signifies the highest levels of Divine activity and creativity. Meditate on *YHVH* for ten minutes.

---

[2] *Outpouring of the Soul (Hishtap 'kuth HaNefesh).* Kaplan, A., trans. Jerusalem: Yishiva Chasidei Breslov, 1980, p. 20.

3) Now focus on *AHYH—Ehyeh*, "I am," or the Hebrew, אהיה . This name is connected with the *sephirah binah*, which signifies Divine harmony and receptivity. Meditate for ten minutes.

4) Now combine the two names together, creating *YAHH-VYHH*, or יאהההויהה . Even though it appears to be nonsense, it signifies the Upper Union of male and female, creativity and harmony, action and reception. Continue your meditation for ten more minutes.

Hebrew Alphabet

In addition to being a mantra, meditating on the names of God can also be mandala meditation. The visual form of each name of God created by Hebrew letters is an object of intense energy. When meditating, the visual form of the name looms up in your consciousness like a giant freeway sign. Through repeated practice, this sign begins appearing everywhere you look and thus God becomes ubiquitous.

Writing at the end of the thirteenth century, Rabbi Jacob HaKohen examined the twenty-two letters of the Hebrew alphabet, their shape, words and phrases beginning with each letter, stories, ideas and feelings associated with them and metaphysical associations. Meditation on each letter produces specific spiritual effects.[3]

Abraham Abulafia (1240-1290), one of the most powerful men in the history of Jewish spiritual teachers, developed an entire system of meditation based upon the magic powers inherent in the Hebrew letters. He advocated writing the letters in a kind of free association and automatic writing. As you half-randomly write letters in hundreds of combinations and permutations you focus the awareness upon the qualities that each letter represents. Abulafia is unusual within the Jewish tradition in that he

---

[3] *The Early Kabbalah*. New York: Paulist Press, 1986, p. 153.

describes his experiences of God most prolificly and in minute detail, from meditation and practice to out of body experience to ecstatic rapture.

In both these systems, the Hebrew letters are more than simply letters. They are essential metaphysical essences that make up the universe, like the elements of chemistry's Periodic Table. The metaphysical significance of letters derives from the *Sefer Yezirah*. *Sefer Yezirah* itself mentions two techniques for using letters as mandalas: "engraving" (Heb. *hakikah*) and "hewing" (Heb. *hatzivah*). Engraving means fixing the image of the letter in your mind, while hewing means removing everything but the letter from your consciousness.[4]

Amulets

For thousands of years, Jews throughout the world have written paper and metal amulets (*Heb. kemaya*) in a particular style. Although primarily used as protective devices against demons, the form of many common amulets shows that they are also pictograms for centering attention. These amulets contain Biblical verses and names of God, usually arranged in a circular pattern, and often including the six-pointed Shield of David.[5]

Two special types of mandala-amulets are common. One is the *mizrah*, "East," and is placed on the wall facing east, the direction one should face when davening, the direction of Jerusalem. The second is a *shiviti*, which means "I have set." Psalm 16:8 reads "I have set *YHVH* always before me."

This line is frequently fashioned into a mandala-amulet and hung on a wall as a constant reminder of the Oneness of God.

---

[4]Kaplan, A. *Jewish Meditation*. New York: Schocken, 1985, p.78.
[5]Schire, T. *Hebrew Magic Amulets*. New York: Behrman House, 1982, plates.

Experience 28

Meditation on a Jewish Mandala

1) If you do not already have one, acquire a six-pointed star, Shield of David (*Heb. magein David*) charm.

2) Reflect on how this charm came into your possession, and what special associations it holds for you.

3) Sit alone in a comfortable place. Relax.

4) Stare at your charm for ten minutes. Focus your gaze so that the charm is the only thing you see.

5) After meditation, reflect on the charm and its significance to you.

❖

Movement and Judaism

Jewish tradition has one major system in which the mind is focused directly on the body. In Abulafia's system of combining the letters of the Hebrew alphabet, each combination has a proper movement and breathing associated with it. In practice, one meditates through 4400 sounds and movements.[6]

Daily davening also possesses a few subtle *hathayoga*-like aspects. During davening there are proper times to sit, stand, cover the eyes (the *Shema*), times to step forward to approach God, times to bow, stand back. In addition, the whole process of davening includes movement of the body, a swinging or swaying, called "*shukkling*." Like *hathayoga,* davening involves the

---

[6]*Or Hasechel (The Light of Insight).* Quoted in Kaplan, A. *Meditation and Kabbalah.* York Beach, Maine: Samuel Weiser, 1982, p. 84.

body in the process, so as to intensify the experience.

Visualizations In Judaism

On first consideration, meditation utilizing visualizations of God, analogous to Tantric materials, seems to be beyond the bounds of what Enlightenment at Sinai will acknowledge. The *Zohar* or *"Book of Splendor,"* the thirteenth century magnum opus of Jewish spiritual experience, however, contains visualizations of God which seem bizarre and heretical. These detailed pictures have a metaphysical significance and describe the interactions of the *sephirot* within the totality of God. In fact, they are a code, describing the male and female elements in God and the physical universe which are inextricably combined in harmonious opposition.[7]

In the Jewish tradition, imagining nothingness is the closest thing to imagining God. The highest of the ten *sephirot* which signifies God's essence is *keter*, the "Crown." Another name for keter is *Ain Sof*, which translates into both "infinity" and "nothingness," both of which are beyond human comprehension. There is no category into which God fits. Even an assertion like "God is love" or "God is spirit" limits God to less than infinity. The only thing one can imagine which is unlimited is nothing.

---

[7]They are not included in the standard ("Sincino") translation of the Zohar, but they are translated elsewhere under the title *The Anatomy of God*, Rosenberg, R., translator, New York: KTAV, 1973.

Experience 29

Meditation on Nothing

1) Sit comfortably in an undisturbed place and relax.
2) Try to make your mind totally blank. Begin by visualizing a blank blackboard. Next visualize the vacuum of outer space. Then realize that even totally empty space is not nothing. Even the perfect vacuum of outer space is a space. Keep your mind focused on absolute nothingness for as long as you can. Even two minutes can be a great challenge.

❖

Anticipating Unfolding

At certain points in Jewish history a particular piece of spiritual activity suddenly becomes very important. The intense spirituality of the 16th Century Luria circle elaborated the rituals to welcome *Shabbat* which had previously been far simpler. Luria's innovations have become so much a part of Jewish practice that it is difficult to imagine Jewish life without them. Such a transformation is beginning to occur in contemporary Jewish life with the infusion of regular meditation.

Chapter 10

Reincarnation

What Was Your Face Before You Were Born?

Reincarnation is an important component of religious life throughout the Far East. In the West, people who believe in reincarnation are often regarded as eccentric, but experiences of past lives are powerful and common, even in a culture as skeptical as ours.

Past lives are something to be "experienced" more than to be "believed in." The brain is "programed" in such a way that it is natural to have the feeling of having lived before and to expereience that past life vividly. The experience is so seemingly real and so powerful that it cannot be swept under the rug with a broom of logical disbelief.

Roberto Assagioli (1888-1974), an early student of Freud and of Jung, described a notion of "subpersonalities," or those psychological traits within an individual which are not fully integrated. According to Assagioli, we act out different subpersonalities in our various roles as spouse, child, parent, worker, friend, supporter.[1] At the very least, a past life experience is the ex-

---

[1] *Psychosynthesis.* New York: Viking, 1971, p. 74-77.

163

perience of an undeveloped subpersonality which had previously been residing in the unconscious, either personal or collective, and exerting subtle influences on the conscious personality.

You may or may not have actually "lived" before. The person you see yourself as having been in a past life may not have been an actual person. However, this person is a real component of the unconscious that effects who you are today. Your feelings, goals, needs, ideals and loves have been influenced by this "being." Becoming conscious of him / her is an important part of spiritual work.

Reincarnation is one of the oldest doctrines in human history. As early as 1500 BCE, the Egyptian Book of the Dead described the transitions of the soul from this life to the next. During transition, the god Osiris promised the soul of the departed that it would incarnate through countless generations to come. The primary reason for the mummification of the body and organs was to keep them available for future use.

In the Far Eastern view, this lifetime is but one stage in a long process of death and rebirth of each immortal soul. Each soul may be millions of years old and may have lived many times already. The soul is a spiritual entity, whose continuity is not dependent upon the individual body it currently happens to inhabit. Its origin is in the Great Oneness, the infinite source of all being. Like a spark from a central fire or a wave that breaks and separates from the ocean, the soul moves out and gathers experience in this physical world, while striving to return to the point of its origin. Each time, the soul attaches itself to a temporary, physical body with a different station in life and different tasks to perform.

The great Eastern scriptures offer paths to release the soul from this cycle. One of religion's central functions is to teach the way out. This life, for all its pleasures and rewards, is a "vale of tears." When a soul is moved to follow a set of teachings and pursues them to their ultimate end, it then reaches its highest level of perfection. Once this has been accomplished, it returns to the Great Oneness where it remains and is not born again.

The cycle of death and rebirth is one of the central themes of the *Upanishads*, the ancient texts upon which Hinduism is founded. The reality of the universe is the equation of *Brahman* with *Atman*. *Brahman* is the Absolute, boundless, impersonal Reality from which all beings and galaxies emerge. The soul of each individual in its essence is *Atman*, the changeless, eternal, universal Self which transmigrates from body to body. *Atman*, however, is not independent and self-contained. It is a unifying entity in which all beings are subsumed together as One.

To realize that *"Atman* equals *Brahman"* is to know the fundamental truth of the universe. This truth can be learned only through an experience of the Oneness of the individual and the Infinite, undifferentiated wholeness of the entire universe. To experience this truth is to realize the human potential for release from further rebirth.

Our actions in this world accumulate karma, the universal "law of cause and effect." Actions in this incarnation determine what will happen later in this lifetime, as well as the form we will take in the next incarnation. The only way out of this cycle is to experience the truth that *Atman* and *Brahman* are one.

The *Bhagavad Gita*, Hinduism's greatest classic, espouses a similar notion. The *Bhagavad Gita* is a dialogue prior to battle between the mortal warrior Arjuna, fearing the suffering his warrioring will cause others, and Krishna, the god who instructs Arjuna that since he is a warrior, he must fulfill that role as best as he is capable. *Karmayoga,* "action taken without attachment," is the ideal toward which the wise direct their energy. *Karmayoga* is the path to break the cycle of further rebirth.

The *Bhagavad Gita* and the *Upanishads* both assume that there is a continuous process of death and rebirth, and that there is a attainable state which will end this cycle. While the *Upanishads* equates it with knowing the Oneness of Atman and Brahman, the *Bhagavad Gita* equates it with selfless action.

Similarly, Buddhism assumes that reincarnation is a metaphysical reality. In Therevada Buddhism, the most ancient Buddhist path, all metaphysical questions, including the transmigration of the soul, are paradoxically neither affirmed nor denied. In Mahayana Buddhism, the most popular Buddhist form, reincarnation is assumed. Gotama Shakyamouni underwent countless incarnations before he attained enlightenment and became known as "The Buddha," "The Fully Enlightened One." Mahayana Buddhist texts record the history of these incarnations and how they contributed to Gotama's elevation to greatness.

According to Mahayana teaching, Buddha was on the threshold of the end of the cycle of death and rebirth when he turned back to this world. He relinquished escape from reincarnation in order to continue teaching others on this earth the substance of his enlightenment. Thus, the ideal of Mahayana Buddhism is not to become an enlightened buddha, but rather to become a "Bodhisattva," "one who renounces full enlightenment in order to aid others."

Taoism, a major component of Chinese religion, supplements Mahayana Buddhism's notion of death and rebirth. The classic writing of Chuang Tzu (c. 300 BCE) relates that:

> Things indeed die and are born, not reaching a perfect state....Man, (at birth) again enters into the great machinery, from which all things come forth...Decay and growth, fullness and emptiness, when they end, begin again. [2]

The Classic Western tradition of Greece and Rome gave reincarnation some credence. The Pythagorean school was reputed to have deemed it one of its central mysteries. Plato affirms reincarnation in his dialogues *Meno* and *Phaedrus,* and concludes *The Republic* with a description of souls choosing their next bodies. In the dialogue *Meno* he writes:

> The soul, then, as being immortal, and having been born again many times, and having seen all things that exist, whether in this world or in the world below...should be able to recall to remembrance all that she ever knew...about everything.

---

[2] Quoted in *Reincarnation*. Head and Cranston, editors. New York: Julain Press, 1977, p. 110.

The Christian tradition began with speculation on reincarnation, but ultimately firmly rejected the idea. A number of early gnostic Christians, such as Basilides, Balentinus, Marcion, and others, were said to be reincarnationists, but their writings have not survived. Origen (185-254 CE) was the most influential theologian of the early church, but his belief in reincarnation was rejected by the church of the Fifth Ecumenical Council of 553 CE. Although a variety of Christian sects, such as gnostic Paulicians, the Manicheans, Catherines, and Albigensians have tried to reestablish reincarnation, mainstream Christianity has resisted it.

The Karma of Jewish Birth

Reincarnation is not a mainstream Jewish view. The Torah assumes an existence of the soul prior to taking on this incarnation. *YHVH* says to the Israelites, "I make this covenant with its sanctions, not with you alone, but both with those here today and those not yet present." (DEUTERONOMY 29:13-14). The Talmud adds that at birth, an angel touches a baby's nose to make it forget that it knows that it comes from God and that it will ultimately return to its source. (B. NIDDAH 30B). The Torah says nothing directly about afterlife. However, in Prophets, God tells the young boy Jeremiah, "Before I even formed you in the belly I knew you, before you emerged from the womb I designated you holy and set you as a prophet to the nations" (JEREMIAH 1:4).

Daniel declares that after a great future catastrophe, "Many of those who sleep in the dust of the earth shall awake, some to everlasting life, and some to shame and everlasting contempt" (DANIEL 12:2).

The *Tanakh* includes a story of King Saul who is worried about the outcome of an upcoming battle (I SAMUEL 28:3f.). He wants to consult Samuel, his deceased prophet, but has himself outlawed all the mediums who might have been able to conjure

Samuel's spirit. He disguises himself and finds a medium, "the woman of Endor." She conjures Samuel, who tells Saul that he will lose the battle and his kingdom to the upstart David. The story demonstrates the Torah's belief that for a brief period after death the soul of the departed lives in the netherworld where its distinct personality remains intact.

The Jewish spiritual path does not spend much time speculating on "what happens after you die." The Jewish emphasis is on this world and what you do here. The tasks of this earth require no afterlife to be validated.

However, the Talmud offers a "classic Jewish view" of the afterlife. Upon death the soul leaves the body, even though body and soul are tenuously connected for the next twelve months, until the body is decomposed. During this year, the soul undergoes a purgatory-like process to cleanse it of the evil karma-like effects it has accrued. After the year, evil souls are destroyed and the righteous go to paradise, the Garden of Eden. Differing opinions hold that the souls of the dead are either "hidden under God's throne," *i.e.* asleep (B. SHABBAT 152b) or fully conscious (EXODUS RABBAH 52:3). Opinions differ about how much the dead know of this world (B. BERAKHOT 18b).

According to this view, at the time when the Messiah comes to Earth, the soul will return to the dust, its body will be reconstituted, and the person will live again. The Messianic Era is a political and physical Utopia. It will last only a few generations, after which history's final epoch, the World-to-Come (Heb. *olam haba*) will begin.

A number of Judaism's teachers have been uncomfortable with the Talmud's insistence that the body is to be resurrected. A cataclysmic upset of the whole world order is difficult to take literally. A body-less immortal soul is a much "neater" notion of afterlife. Therefore, the Talmud's resurrection has often been reinterpreted to mean that the soul itself is immortal and does not need the body to retain consciousness after death. The great Jewish teacher of the tenth century, Sa'adia Gaon (892-942 CE) described this resurrected state as a condition of "spiritual bliss" (*Book of Beliefs and Opinions* 9:5) rather than restored physical vitality.

The nineteenth century founders of liberal Judaism were also uncomfortable with the Talmudic view of physical resurrection. The Pittsburgh Platform of 1885, the first statement of principles of the Reform Movement in the United States, de-supernaturalizes the Messianic age as "...the establishment of the kingdom of truth, justice and peace among all men." The resurrection of the body is unambiguously exchanged for the immortality of the soul.

Many of the most important Jewish teachers have ignored, denied and even ridiculed the possibility of reincarnation. Sa'adia Gaon wrote that he found "certain people, who call themselves Jews, professing the doctrine of reincarnation...and other such nonsense and stupidities" (*Beliefs and Opinions*, 6:8). Among our preeminent sages, Maimonides and Yehudah Halevi (1080-1141) do not even mention reincarnation. The philosopher Joseph Albo (1380-1444) rejects it outright.

Nevertheless, there are some teachers who have argued for reincarnation. Anan ben David, the eighth century founder of Karaism, an important Jewish sect, is the earliest proponent of reincarnation, though his own sect later rejected his view.

Sefer HaBahir, "The Book of Radiance" (twelfth century), which was widely studied throughout Europe for several hundred years, takes reincarnation for granted:

> What does it mean, "One generation passes away and another generation comes? (ECCLESIASTES 1:4)...A parable: A king had servants and dressed them according in clothes of silk. The servants went astray. So he cast them out, and took off their clothes and washed them well. He acquired new servants and dressed them in those garments. Thus they took part in garments which had already been in existence and worn by others" (*Sefer HaBahir*, No. 86).

In other words, the immortal soul (garment) goes from body to interchangeable body.

According to the *Zohar*, the soul has to endure up to six incarnations until it is released to return to God-Its-Source. Furthermore, the *Zohar* maintains that reincarnation explains the
genesis of converts to Judaism: they were Jewish souls mistakenly attached to non-Jewish bodies (II:95B).

In the fourteenth century, the doctrine of reincarnation spread
through the Jewish world. According to the Torah, if a man dies
without children, his brother must wed his widow and their children bear the deceased brother's name (DEUTERONOMY 25:5). The
reincarnational explanation for this practice was that the soul of
the dead brother reincarnated in the body of his nephew/son.[3]

Reincarnation also was used to account for the apparent suffering of the righteous and the prospering of the wicked in this
world. A righteous person can be punished for his or her sins
in a previous incarnation. The sufferings of Job, particularly, were
understood in light of multiple lifetimes of the soul. Rabbi Moshe
ben Naḥman (Nachmanides, 1194-1270), wrote a commentary
to Job, in which the mystery of reincarnation was the key to the
implied meaning of Job's suffering.[4]

The most elaborate Jewish explication of reincarnation was developed by Isaac Luria and his circle in Safed. They maintained
that transmigration occurs in all forms of existence, from the
sephirot themselves through angels, human beings, animals and
inorganic matter. Everything is constantly changing form,
descending to the lowest form and ascending again to the highest.
Furthermore, there are a limited number of root souls, from
which many individual souls branch out. All the souls with the
same root origin have common characteristics and similar life
tasks. Biblical events are understood through this lens. For example, Moses and his father-in-law Yitro are reincarnations of
Cain and Abel, with thousand-year-old family conflicts to resolve.
Adam, Eve, and the serpent, the archetypal couple and inter-

---

[3]Scholem, G. *The Kabbalah.* New York: Quadrangle/New York Times, 1974, p. 345.
[4]Chavel. *The Writings of Nahmanides.* Jerusalem, Shilo, 1963, Vol. I, p. 347.

loper, reincarnate into David, Batsheva and Uriah (II SAMUELS 11) in an attempt to repair the original damage.[5]

Ḥayyim Vital, the student-scribe who preserved Luria's teachings, wrote that each soul must continue to reincarnate until it has fulfilled all 613 *miẓvot*.[6]

The great teachers of the Hasidic movement assumed the reality of reincarnation. Hasidic penitential prayer asked God to pardon one's sins in previous incarnations. Hasidic legend relates that Rabbi Abraham Joshua Heschel of Opatow (d. 1825) could remember that in a previous incarnation he had been the High Priest in the Temple. During *Yom Kippur* service, where the ritual in the Temple was described, he would read "Thus did I say," rather than "Thus did he [the High Priest] say."[7]

The classic Talmudic view of Jewish afterlife is generally assumed to be echoed in the second benediction of The *Prayer*, a central component of every davening. This paragraph praises God for "trustfully keeping his promise to those who sleep in the dust," and the benediction's conclusion praises God "who revives the dead."

However, The *Prayer* can just as easily be understood as affirmation of reincarnation:

> You are infinitely strong, *Adonai*,
> You reincarnate the dead with your great saving power.
> You sustain life with *ḥesed*.
> You reincarnate the dead with your boundless compassion.
> Supporter of the fallen, healer of the sick, and unbinder of the captive,
> And keeper of that promise to those sleeping in the dust.
> Who is like You, strongest of all,
> And who is Your equal?

---

[5][6]Scholem, G. *op. cit. p. 347.*

[7]*Sefer HaGilgulim*, quoted in *The Secret Garden*. Meltzer, D., editor, New York: Seabury, 1976, p. 129f.

[8]Jacobs, L. *What Does Judaism Say About...?*. New York: Quadrangle/New York Times, 1973, p. 276.

Ruler who causes life and rebirth, and whose saving power springs
eternal.
You will faithfully reincarnate the dead,
Praised are you, *Adonai*, who reincarnates the dead.

Throughout all of these references to reincarnation in Jewish
tradition, there is the recurrent understanding that Jews are usually reincarnated as Jews, non-Jews as non-Jews. The noteworthy
few non-Jews who embrace Judaism are seen to have Jewish souls
that were somehow lost.

There is a particular karma of being born Jewish. Karma is
not predetermination. Rather, it means that our particular set
of opportunities has been caused by past actions. What we make
of those opportunities is at the discretion of free will.

If you were born a Jew, there probably reside in your unconscious a few subpersonalities, archetypes or memories of previous
Jewish incarnations. The major events of Jewish history are not
just stories you heard as a child. They are engraved deeply in
your psyche. If you are a non-Jew who feels attracted to Judaism, this too may be a result of previous incarnations.

Experience 30

Why Were You (or Weren't You) Born Jewish?

1) Sit comfortably in a quiet place, relax.

2) Meditate on the question of "Why was I born Jewish?" or
"Why wasn't I born Jewish?" Ask yourself the question over and
over. As each answer emerges, note it and place it aside. Return
to asking the question. Continue for at least 5 minutes.

3) At the end of your meditation, write down all the answers
that seem significant to you.

❖

Reincarnation and Evil

The most attractive feature of a belief in reincarnation is that it solves the "problem of evil." If God is powerful and good, why does God permit undeserved pain and suffering? If this lifetime is not the end of a soul's journey, then suffering of the innocent is only apparent suffering. The child who dies with great agony is accumulating karma in his or her journey that traverses many lifetimes.

The greatest current Jewish difficulty in moving to embrace reincarnation is that it seems to conflict with Judiasm's dearly held notion of this lifetime's supreme importance. In fact, however, reincarnation only moderates the importance of this lifetime very slightly. Even in the face of our greatest national catastrophes, the Jewish path has insisted that our pains are part of God's plan and our existence has meaning. Reincarnation provides a broader scope in which to find that plan and meaning.

Chapter 11

Judaism and Christianity

Why Judaism Rejects Jesus' Messiahship

Although we have been looking at the Jewish path from the vantage point of the Far East, most Jewish spirituality has unfolded in the Christian West.

The Jewish-Christian encounter has effected important aspects of Jewish spirituality, and their interrelationship has been problematic for both religions.

Jung's theory of the archetype helps illuminate why it has been difficult. The Jewish notion of Messiah tends to be "this world-ly," as "this worldly-ness" is an important feature of all aspects of Judaism. Jewish expectation of the Messiah (Heb. *mashiah*) includes a restoration of all the Jewish people to national independence in their own land and an inauguration of an age of world peace.

Literally, the Messiah is a military and/or political figure who effects majors changes in the life of the Jewish tribe, while the miraculous resurrection of everyone who ever lived righteously commences. Figuratively, the Messiah is a future era when human beings throughout the world live together in peace. Spiritually, the coming of the Messiah means the internal experience of God.

For the last 2000 years, Judaism has insisted that no Messiah has yet come. Most of the Jewish world has coexisted within predominantly Christian cultures, which claim that Jesus was the Jewish Messiah whose mission spawned Christianity.

In addition, Christianity determined that its own existence made Torah null and void and that the Jewish spiritual path of *mizvot*, and *halakhah* is worthless. The result of this conviction has been 2000 years of anti-Semitism.

Christianity, anti-Semitism, archetype, and the Holocaust form an inseparable complex. In order to unravel this complex, one must consider Christianity's 2000-year old challenge to Judaism: Why isn't Jesus the Jewish Messiah?

The considerable political and religious instability of Jesus's day, combined with a public perception of religion as overinstitutionalized and spiritually poor, created a climate for a charismatic young leader for change to emerge. As religious institutions mature, spiritual experience frequently takes second place to institutional stability. Every human institution, if it is to endure and mature, needs periodic fine tuning of its routines and image.

Though Jesus tried to fit the definition of Messiah through his political activities, he did not fulfill the traditional Jewish messianic hopes of national redemption. He neither restored the ancient glories of Israel nor did he usher in an age of universal peace.

After Jesus' death, Christianity emerges with an alternate notion of messianship, based upon the events of Jesus' death and resurrection. For Jews to have joined in this transformation from national aspiration to a universal spiritual movement, Jesus would have needed to show more respect for the subtleties of Torah.

However, the Gospels depict Jesus in constant opposition to the Jewish leadership of his day, which is painted as ignorant, decrepit, egotistical and spiritually dead. In contrast, Jesus is shown to be wise, charismatic and endowed with miraculous abilities. The Pharisees, the recognized Rabbinic leadership of Je-

sus' day, are shown repeatedly to be an odious lot who miss the
obvious wisdom of Jesus' simple teachings. In fact, however, the
Pharisees were intensely spiritual. Their own literature, the
Talmud, shows that these Rabbis lived every moment of their
lives with God in their consciousness. They themselves were miracle workers and sacred technicians of great talent.

Yet, throughout the Gospel, Jesus confounds and confronts
the Pharisees. He quotes Scripture to them in challenge to their
authority. He rejects Torah's demands in both obvious and subtle ways. For example, *halakhah* demands that all healing should
be postponed until *Shabbat* is over, unless life is endangered.
It is important that healers themselves have the opportunity to
experience *Shabbat*. Jesus violated this principle:

> ...They asked Jesus, "Is it permitted to heal on *Shabbat*?" He said
> to them, "...Surely it is permitted to do good on *Shabbat*." Turning
> to the man he said, "Stretch out your arm." He stretched it out, and
> it was made strong again like the other." (MATTHEW 12:9-14; see also LUKE
> 6:6-11; 14:3-6; JOHN 15:16)

The Torah's laws of marriage and divorce enhance the stability of Jewish communities. *Halakhah* is realistic: it permits but
discourages divorces in a wide latitude of situations. Jesus opposed these liberal laws:

> If a man divorces his wife for any cause other than unchastity he
> involves her in adultery; and anyone who marry a divorced woman com-
> mits adultery (MATTHEW 5:31-32)

In the first example, Jesus is a tradition-basher in order to help
people, and in the second he's the ultraconservative making life
more difficult for the liberals. Together, they indicate the Christian Scriptures wanted to make it clear that they already drew
a line between themselves and their roots.

Jesus ate meals in places where *kashrut* was not observed (MAT-
THEW 9:10-13). He defends himself saying that he must eat with
the nonobservant in order to teach them. *Halakhah* maintains
the preeminence of spiritual discipline, and that *halakhah* itself
is the most important matter to teach. Furthermore, one teaches

best by example.

One of the Torah's *miẓvot* is to wash hands before eating. Jesus ignored this ritual (MATTHEW 15:12), and he desecrated Jewish fast days (MATTHEW 9:14f, MARK 2:18-20, LUKE 5:33-35). He counselled people to shun communal Jewish worship, a powerful component of Jewish spirituality:

> When you pray, do not be like the hypocrites; they love to say their prayers standing up in the synagogue....When you pray, go into a room by yourself, shut the door, and pray to your Father who is there in the secret place... (MATTHEW 6:5)

Yet Jesus, like Mohammed, took the essence of the experience of the Oneness of God and modified it to a form that captured the spiritual inclinations of much of the world's population. The spread of Christianity indicates how closely Jesus conforms to an archetypal expectation: the god who becomes human and suffers in order to give human suffering meaning. The original Jewish rendition of that archetype as the god who appears without form is more subtle and more difficult.

In addition, Christianity's success resulted in no small measure from the ritual of the Eucharist: the primary sacrificial meal where God appears and enters within the body and soul of each communicant. It is one of the most powerful means to facilitate the experience of God ever devised.

On the Jewish spiritual path, the Messiah has not yet come. In the meantime, we get a few hints of what the internal spiritual transformation of the Messiah's coming will be like. At the *havdalah* ceremony which marks the conclusion of *Shabbat*, Elijah, the prophet who never died and who will return to announce the Messiah's coming, is present for one moment. That moment is neither part of *Shabbat* nor part of the six other days of the week. It is a moment outside of time, a foretaste of the experience of ultimate spiritual fulfillment. Similarly, Elijah appears with his momentary Messianic foretaste at the conclusion of the *Pesaḥ seder* celebration. The original 'Letting Go of Egypt' was a moment outside of time. Each annual celebration of that event also includes a moment outside of time.

The Jewish spiritual path is a path of waiting, of anticipating what is yet to come. Until the Messiah comes, there is much spiritual work to be done.

Archetypal Anti-Semitism

By reflecting the conflict between Jesus and the Jewish leaders of his day, the Christian Scriptures created a negative archetype of the Jew which is the central underlying cause of two millenia of anti-Semitism.

An archetype is an image which comes out of the collective unconscious. An archetype serves as a base line pattern with which the mind organizes its experience. Seemingly unrelated feelings values, yearnings and ideals are organized into the concrete form of archetypal characters. These characters are celebrated as the heroes and villians of their culture. As such the archetypes create and enforce what the culture desires.

We are unable to perceive our own experience without projecting the archetype upon it. We feel the urge to overcome an obstacle, and so identify with the hero. Without such archetypes, our vague urges would not take concrete form.

Problems result when the feelings stimulated by the archetype cannot be distinguished from the external world. For instance, we may have genuine adversaries in life who threaten our well being. But if our fear of an archetypal enemy is applied to a real person, however benign, we may cause needless harm to an innocent individual.

One of the key elements in Jung's psychology is the archetype of the Shadow. Analogous to Freud's *id*, the Shadow is the dark side of the human personality. The Shadow includes those aspects of a person which are repressed into the unconscious because their content is not acceptable to the conscious mind, the uncivilized desires and emotions that cannot be expressed. However, the Shadow manages to find its own means of expression, often by ascribing to others those characteristics which the individual most strongly denies. The archetype of the Shadow gives birth to the many negative aspects of the archetype of the Jew.

The Gospels paint a picture of Jesus' conflict with the Jews of his day which reflects the times, or that of a generation later when they were edited. Whether the picture of the Jews is accurate or propaganda, it has informed the Christian perception of Jews and Judaism ever since.

According to Christian mythology, Christianity is the "New Israel" which replaces Judaism, the "Old Israel." Paul asserts that Christians are the true "Israel of God" (GALATIANS 6:16), that guidance from Torah "condemns to death" (II CORINTHIANS 3:6), and that Jews "were lopped off for lack of faith (ROMANS 11:20). Paul even writes *Midrash* to argue that Jews are actually descendants of Abraham's son, Ishmael, born by the slave Hagar, while those who believe in Jesus are the true descendants of Isaac and the recipients of the blessings promised Abraham (GALATIANS 4:22-31).

Due to Jesus' frequent invectives against the scribes and Pharisees (*e.g.* MATTHEW 3; LUKE 11:37-53; MARK 12:38-40) "Pharisee" has become a derogatory epithet. In the Jewish tradition, however, "Pharisee" is a badge of honor, a term of respect for scholars of Torah. Jesus' laxness about *kashrut,* his rejection of ritual purifications, his aversion to synagogues stamp these practices and institutions as abhorrent and petty to the Christian mind.

Christian myth carries an irony: Judaism is the root from which Christianity grew. Rather than respecting these roots, the Christian Scriptures show scorn for the Jewish people and their religion. In John's Gospel particularly, the very word "Jew" is a synonym for a variety of negative traits, even though Jesus and his disciples were Jewish.

This negative image of Judaism is a direct result of Christianity's Jewish roots, coupled the charge of deicide. In the Christian myth, the Jew is responsible for bringing God to life, and then for killing God.

Any moral or ethical code demands that its followers repress some of their natural instincts for a higher good. When this repressed energy gets too strong to contain, something boils over, creating violent or anti-social behavior.

In the Christian myth, the demands of God originated with the Jew. By contrast, pre-Christian paganism, whether Teutonic, Hellenic, Slavic or Latin celebrates the unbridled, physical joys of this world. The Jew introduced the One God who demands restraint. Thus, the Jew is responsible for all repression and the target of the resultant bottled-up anger.

At the same time, the Jew has killed God and taken God away. The most destructive invective against Judaism has been the charge of deicide, "killer of God," as expressed in these words:

> So when Pilate saw that he was gaining nothing, but rather that a riot was beginning, he took water and washed his hands before the crowd, saying, 'I am innocent of this man's blood. Take it upon yourselves.' And all the people answered, 'His blood be on us and our children.' Then he...delivered [Jesus] to be crucified (MATTHEW 27:24-26).

Thus, it proclaimed the Jew to be the embodiment of ultimate power and evil, for the Jew has the will and ability to kill God. Until Vatican II, barely twenty-five years ago, the Jews' responsibility for Jesus' death was an accepted part of Christian theology and caused untold Jewish suffering.

By rejecting Jesus as messiah, the Jew rejects the only path to salvation which Christianity recognizes. The Jew forfeits salvation and stands as a threat to others who might be tempted to do the same. The Jew is disgraced in this world and eternally damned in the next.

The Archetype of Jew in Western Culture

Archetypes manifest themselves as myth, in dreams, and as motifs in a culture's art forms. The negative archetype of Jew has been ubiquitous in Western art and literature. From the medieval period to the present, the leitmotifs of the demonic, greedy and vanquished Jew are on stage, in the cathedral, and in the printed word.

The mystery plays of the Middle Ages frequently present Satan inciting Jews against Jesus and conspiring with them to kill him. In the famous French drama, *La Mystère de la Passion*, the Jews and the devil conspire to entice Judas to betray Jesus, and they howl with glee at their own success. In the Charmont Christmas play, Jews are introduced on stage in the guise of the devil, struggling to prevent entrance of a religious procession into the city. In an era which was almost totally illiterate and virtually devoid of mass media influences, religious dramas like these were the major source of religious instruction, as well as popular entertainment.[1]

There are medieval AntiChrist plays which stressed the relation between the AntiChrist and the Jew. The AntiChrist's life story was an inverted burlesque of Jesus' career. The child of a Jewish prostitute and Satan, at age thirty he reveals himself to the Jews as their messiah. The master of black magical arts, his ministry last three and half years until he attempts to ape Jesus' final achievement and ascend to heaven borne by demons. The archangel Michael is dispatched to destroy him. His Jewish followers are annihilated, the world comes to an end, and Jesus comes back to earth.[2]

Another aspect of the archetypal Jew myth is the "host desecration." According to traditional Christian theology, the communion wafers actually become the body of Jesus. In this myth, the wafers come into Jewish hands. The Jew mutilates the host, blood flows from it, and a miraculous event occurs, usually harming the Jew. The Jew is apprehended and executed along with any other Jews the mob can lay its hands on. This theme became one of the most popular subjects of medieval literature, and it

---

[1]Tractenberg, I. *The Devil and The Jews*. New York: Harper and Row, 1966, p. 22-23.
[2]Ibid p. 35-36.

found frequent expression in 15th and 16th century woodcuts. From Prague in 1389 comes the story of an attack by Jews upon a monk carrying the hosts, in which the Jews are alleged to have taunted, "You have the Lord God in your hands; let him protect you." Some 3,000 Jews were executed in reprisal. In 1453, Jews of Breslau are reported to have confessed, under torture, that they stole the host, "...to see whether God was really in it."

Shylock reflects the negative Jewish archetype, but Shakespeare's artistic subtlety makes him a far more complex character. Shylock's demand for his pound of flesh only comes after he has been utterly victimized for four acts. His loss of his daughter and fortune, coupled with his forced conversion ends the play by engaging our sympathy.

Similarly, the ritual murder accusation, the charge that Jews require the blood of a Christian in their religious rituals, particularly for the celebration of *Pesah* (Passover), was one of the most pervasive features of medieval religious life. Over 150 "substantiated" charges of ritual murder are listed in standard reference works. Chaucer's Canterbury Tales includes "The Prioress's Tale" which repeats this "blood accusation." Significantly, this tale is told by an official of the Church. So strong was the Christian belief that ritual murder was a requirement of Jewish law that vengeance was an annual event during the Passover-Easter season.

The host desecration and the blood libel both occur at the Passover-Easter season. This season was the time of year when the Jews were responsible for Jesus' death. Jesus' last supper was a celebration of the *Pesah seder* meal. The first Christian communion was a reinterpretation of the *mizvah* to eat unleavened bread (*mazah*) and to drink wine during the festival. Nevertheless, Christian theologians came to interpret the *mazah* and wine of the *Pesah seder* themselves as desecration of the host. Throughout the centuries, many Jews have died as a result.

Another archetypal variation is the Wandering Jew, condemned by Jesus to wander the earth forever for having rebuffed Jesus on his way to the crucifixion. Over one hundred folktales of the Wandering Jew have been collected from the 13th to the 20th centuries, from the Ukraine to the United States. In modern literature, this motif has been used by Shelley, Gorki, Hans Christian Anderson, Goethe, Kipling, and Hawthorne.

Finally, no overview of the archetype of Jew variations is complete without mention of the twin female figures, Ecclesia and Synagoga. This pair of statues prominently graces many of the European cathedrals and countless illuminated manuscripts. They symbolize the Church triumphant and the Synagogue rejected and fallen. Ecclesia is a proud but modest maid, erect and triumphant, holding a cross. Synagoga is a blindfolded harlot, holding a broken staff or broken tablets symbolizing Torah.

Archetypes and Annihilation

The power of archetypes is very real. The archetype of Jew has been responsible for centuries of pogroms, massacres, rapes and murders. At virtually every juncture of Western history there is a Judeophobic subcurrent.

For example, consider the Crusades. In school, we all learned how they were launched to liberate the Holy Land from the Moslems. However, at least as important was the desire to open trade with the Middle East to the rising Christian middle class. Previously, Jews were the principle merchants along that commercial route. The participants of the First Crusade murdered thousands of Jews along their trek and took whatever wealth Jewish traders had as ransom to save themselves.

Jews had become traders in the first place because Jews were forbidden to own land, to become citizens, or to participate in most of the lucrative trades in almost every country in which they lived. Expulsion was such an everpresent reality that trading skills, the most easily transferable from one homebase to another, became the most common Jewish profession. In this framework, liquid assets are always preferable to material goods. As the Christian peasants typically had no money, Jews became the first urban middle class. Jewish traders became "money lenders," that is to say, bankers, when the trade route was closed to them. Although a few Jews did manage to become quite wealthy through this arrangement, even the most wealthy were vulnerable to whatever ransoms dissolvent nobles might demand.

Jews lent large sums to the Christian nobles to finance the First Crusade. A few decades later, the major motivation used by rulers to get their vassals to join the Second Crusade was to promise annulment of debts to Jews acquired at the First Crusade.

Important "progressive" Western thinkers, like Martin Luther, Voltaire, and Karl Marx were not immune to the power of the archetype of the Jew. Each of them wrote rabid anti-Semitic tracts. The Renaissance, The Ukrainian Revolution of 1648, the European Revolutions of 1848, and the transition from Leninism to Stalinism in the Soviet Union were all fueled by this archetype.

The Nazi Holocaust of World War II was the most horrible chapter of anti-Semitism's sorry history. Nazism drew upon this Christian anti-Semitic tradition and carried it to its logical, horrible conclusion. Nazism added one new element: it harnassed all the available technology of its day to deliberately murder Jews by the millions.

There have been many great catastrophes where thousands and even hundreds of thousands have died. The Soviet Union lost more individuals during World War II than the number of Jews destroyed in the Holocaust. Stalin's death camps worked uncounted millions, including hundreds of thousands of Jews, to their deaths. There have been many wars in which one side murdered countless thousands of civilians, needlessly. The Khmer Rouge have usurped the mantle of the Turks as most ruthless in this regard. Hiroshima and Nagasaki obliterated hundreds of thousands in a moment. However, no one but the Nazis built gas chambers where so many were systematically rounded up, transported and efficiently murdered, for no cause other than their birth.

Anti-Semitism prior to the Holocaust was less calculated, but

Nazism had many precedents to draw upon. The Nazis publicly burned books by Jewish authors in 1933; that had been done by Saint Louis IX of France in 1242. The Nazis made Jews wear a yellow star; that had been invented by Pope Innocent III in 1215. The Nazis restricted Jewish commerce to the ghetto; that had been decreed by Pope Pius IV during the "Age of Enlightenment" in 1775. The Nazis burned Jews alive by lighting fires in packed synagogues, an activity invented by the Crusaders when they conquered Jerusalem in 1099. Even the ultimate death decree, the infamous "Final Solution to the Jewish Problem," had its roots in Europe's code words, "Jewish problem," for the question of the extent to which Jews should be allowed rights as citizens.

To the Nazis, the archetype of Jew was real and resulted in a mass neurosis which infected all of Germany and much of Eastern Europe for decades. Archetypes survive hundreds of years, constantly distorting reality. However, the power of an archetype can be diffused if subjected to analysis. In personal analysis, this means a period of intense, deep introspection spent looking at the archetype, coming to terms with its effects, and learning to live without its domination. On a cultural level, diffusing an archetype requires a prolonged period of group-wide introspection, admission of the archetype's existence and the harm it has caused, and resolution to work toward its elimination.

Few Christian clergy and laity have acknowledged Christianity's role in the history of anti-Semitism, including the Holocaust. There are a few who have: Franklin Littell, Rosemary Reuther, James Harry Cargas, Eugene Fisher, and John Pawlikowski. They are voices crying in the wilderness. Most Christian thinkers pay lip-service to the horrors of the Holocaust without recognizing the fact that anti-Semitism has been a salient feature of Christianity since its inception.

The Holocaust teaches us that 1900 years of European Christian spiritual experience has been, in a certain real sense, a failure. Christianity, the dominate moderating spiritual force in Europe, was unable to do much in opposition to this human depravity. There were elements in various churches who opposed Nazism, but their ability to temper the Nazi onslaught was almost nil. Those Christians who acted to oppose Nazism or who took great personal risks to save Jews were, unfortunately, rare exceptions. Generations of preaching about the power of Christian love were of no avail against this ultimate evil.

The Christianization of Europe did not restrain Germans and also Poles, Ukranians, Serbs, Roumanians, and more, from engaging in this barbarity. There were even clergy throughout Europe who gave the Nazis their wholehearted support. There were thousands of professing Christians who took part in the massacres. Christianity's inability to prevent the Holocaust shows the minimal penetration of Christianity's spiritual side into the psyche of most Europeans. Even if the murderers were outside of their churches, they grew up in an environment whose celebrations, ethics and values were Christian. Christianity's inability to temper the behavior of so many testifies to the weakness of Christian spirituality when opposed by the power of the archetype.

Until Christianity can admit its role in the history of anti-Semitism, it will be stifled by its own hidden, destructive components and by the guilt it carries for its past actions. If a spiritual tradition is to lead its followers close to God, it must reject needless violence and it must be honest about the violence it has caused. The unbroken and unrecognized complex of Christian Scripture, Archetype of the Jew, Anti-Semitism, and Holocaust creates a very real chasm between Christian and God-consciousness, and leaves open the possibility of further catastrophic anti-Semitism.

Chapter 12

Lessons We've Learned

Contemporary Reemerging Spirituality

The need and desire for direct, intense, personal experience of God is a universal phenomenon that is becoming more manifest in the most advanced technological and scientific culture ever known, our own. The need for God cuts across all socioeconomic and religious segments of American culture. While this need doesn't affect everyone, there is a growing minority who feel an ancient inclination to connect totally to the Source of Being. An expanding intuition says it is the single most important thing to do on this Earth. Seeking the experience of God is part of the archetypal psychic makeup of every human being.

A trip to any bookstore will reveal the extent to which spirituality is an important area of exploration and fascination. The number of ancient spiritual texts and guides to old traditions published in recent years is astounding. Vastly different forms of spirituality, from Shirley MacLean's best sellers, translations of Buddhist sutras, and Joseph Campbell's guides to mythology, all appeal to different subsets of the spiritually inclined minority. Ancient oracles, tools of the sacred technician like Tarot, astrology, the *I Ching*, and Celtic runes are described in dozens of new publications each month.

As a result of this trend, some suggest that spiritual awareness is increasing because of a planetary, evolutionary transformation, and that this transformation will have the greatest
significance upon the next phase of history as we move toward
peace and light.

The technological age has itself facilitated this growth by allowing the spiritual traditions of the world to get acquainted with
each other for the first time in human history. Whereas until
modern times one or two prophets, avatars, or perfect masters
might emerge within each culture's generation, we now live in
the global village. Spiritual teachers can communicate with each
other and with the masses in ways never before imagined.

The Jewish experience has been that of one small tribe which
has clung tenaciously to its own survival. It has had enormous
impact on every culture with which it has been in contact, in
part because of its conviction that its own historic experience of
God is unique and powerful.

The rising interest in spirituality urges the Jewish tradition to
take another look at itself and to consider once again what has
always been its own essence: the quest for the experience of God.

The Jewish experience teaches that the world is relatively static. New forces do no evolve quickly. The Jewish experience has
seen many religious and spiritual forces come and go since the
dawn of civilization. Many movements have proclaimed that the
world is undergoing a transformation and that everything will
soon be better. This is not the first time that a movement has
claimed to be motivated by a new spiritual awakening throughout the planet.

Movements that proclaim some sort of essential transformation of the planet have a "messianic" character. There have been
a long procession of Jews and nonJews who claimed to be or were
touted as the Messiah. There have been many social movements
which promised a global transformation. By now, we have learned
to be very careful about the next new Messiah that comes down

the road. The Talmud teaches that if you are planting a tree and someone tells you that the Messiah has come, finish planting the tree and then go greet the Messiah.

However, the interaction of contemporary technology, particularly communications technology, with ancient spirituality is creating a world-wide situation without precedent. The extent of this change and its significance is still an open question.

Monotheism and Paganism

Judaism's greatest contribution to the history of the world has been an unshakable commitment to monotheism: the central idea that God is One. In Hebrew, the Oneness of God is called *ha-ikkar*, "The Principle." Judaism replaced paganism whose central experience includes a variety of gods. There do seem to be powers in the natural world, diverse spirits who guide the destinies of people, places and things. Often the differing powers seem to struggle with one another. Some of these powers can be controlled with the proper rituals or attitudes. Some are more evasive. There may be a deep level at which all powers are acknowledged to be differing manifestations of a single unity, but paganism puts a clear emphasis upon the variety of powers.

When Christianity supplanted the various paganisms of the West, it also steamrollered the truth that they expressed: that the world is a magical place, alive with a variety of powers, sometimes harmonious, sometimes acrimonious, but always making life wonderfully fascinating. In the pagan view, each lover is a gift of Aphrodite, each thunderstorm Zeus' wrath, each growing season a tribute to Apollo. The renewed interest in the mythologies of the world pays homage to this diversity.

Since the experience of God is an experience of the *neshamah*, the Higher Self, spiritual traditions sometimes confuse the Higher Self or the manifestation of God-Within with the totality of God. According to Torah, each individual is "created in the image of God," but God is more that the individual and more than the sum total of all individuals. Each individual reflects a facet of God's totality.

In the final analysis, monotheism is a more profound expression of human experience than paganism. The essential oneness of the universe is intuitively known by the psyche of each individual. The oneness of God is reflected in the oneness of the soul of the individual. The lessor gods and powers of nature are subservient spirits whose permission to exist derives from the one great power that permeates and animates all things in the universe.

From a Jewish perspective, if you pay too much homage to a minor power without clearly affirming that God is One, then you have reverted to paganism and the experience of the Oneness of God will become distant from you. Paganism is attractive because it fits many superficial observations of human experience. However, at a deep intuitive level, affirmed Oneness is a far more profound and more spiritual expression of the sublime.

The Here and Now

Judaism is unique among the major religions of the world in its awareness that this world and this lifetime are of paramount importance. Judaism grasped long ago that the hard realities of this world are the only things we know with any certainty. Future life is a delightful long shot and past lives may determine who we have been up to now. But neither diminishes the number one, most essential task of each individual in this world: to find the path and do the work that will transform this lifetime into the ultimate human experience.

Torah insists that the continuity of a spiritual path depends upon the continuity of a community which values it. The community needs a very clear sense of what is just and right if it is to survive, and it must translate that sense into actions. Actions are more powerful than feelings. On the Jewish path, the highest karma of all is accrued through martyrdom (*Heb. kiddush haShem*). Martyrdom is the ultimate act: sacrificing ones own life to inspire the community to the importance of continuing its spiritual work.

Love and Rightness

The path of Torah resists the temptation of declaring "unconditional love" to be the principle manifestation of God. Torah recognizes that love is too nebulous a formulation to declare an absolute. Love must be balanced by "rightness" (Heb. *zedek*). The *sephirot* of the right side balance the *sephirot* of the left, as *halakhah* translates this equilibrium into specific acts of spiritual transformation.

In any given situation, there are a variety of factors at work, and there is always more than one possible course of action. Often, more than one of these choices appears to be a manifestation of love. Is it a greater act of love to allow a dangerous criminal to remain free, or to keep him or her incarcerated? Ultimately, love without "rightness" can only multiply suffering.

Torah is founded upon love, but it is love tempered by a realistic appraisal of the world as evidenced through centuries of experience. Even the love of God is appropriately tempered by the awe of God.

The Metaphysics of Suffering

The current century has seen evil of greater proportions than we would have dreamed possible in a so-called modern world. But the veneer of civilization is thin and human capacity for evil and destruction is great. At this time, evidence of global spiritual transformation is tentative, though encouraging. There is growing awareness among people that the world is indeed becoming a global village and that new sensitivities must develop to assure human survival.

Ironically, and perhaps ominously, Germany in the late 1920's and early 1930's experienced a similar burst of interest in mythology and metaphysics. During this period, Germany was one of the most liberal countries in the West. Its very openness, however, left it vulnerable to forces which utterly overpowered its higher impulses. Nazism itself appropriated a great deal of metaphysical vocabulary which it twisted to murderous ends.

Making sense out of the Holocaust is the ultimate challenge to Jewish spirituality. Jewish tradition has always maintained that whatever occurs on this earth is an expression of God's will: Nothing happens by accident; even the most terrible events are manifestations of God's pattern. However, it staggers the imagination to come up with an explanation for the monstrous pain and suffering which an active, All-powerful, Loving God could permit.

Since 1945, Jewish thinkers have agonized trying to find an explanation. There are theories that God is no longer active and personal, but only an impersonal holy nothingness. Other scholars argue that God's powers are limited or simply an anthropomorphic force. Still others apologize for God, and forgive God for allowing a remnant of Jews to be saved. The concept of reincarnation offers another solution, if not solace: God permitted the Holocaust because the life of a person, even the lives of six million, cannot be limited to one incarnation. Each individual martyr was in the process of death and rebirth which transcends each individual lifetime.

The most radical lesson of Jewish suffering is this: even in light of the Holocaust, the attraction of the experience of God has not diminished. God is not so much what one "believes in." God is what one experiences. The primary intuition, the thirst of the soul to experience its source, is not diminished by the pains of the real world. The path to the experience of God gives life meaning, even in spite of the most horrible suffering imaginable.

Yet on a certain level, any effort to rationalize the sufferings of the Holocaust still sounds insensitive at best, like blasphemy at worst. Through 4000 years of Jewish spirituality on this planet, we have learned certain lessons. Though we have suffered, and we have been challenged to make sense of that suffering, we have not yet reached Buddha's conclusion that "All life is suffering."

Jewish History and Synchronicity

There is a story told that a famous king was asked to give the best proof he knew for the existence of God. He replied, "The survival of the Jews."

Of all Jung's insights, perhaps the one most difficult for the Western mind to affirm is the concept of synchronicity. Occasionally, certain seemingly unrelated events occur at the same time in so bizarre a manner as to defy rational explanation. The overwhelming reliability of diverse oracles testifies that sometimes events unfold as though a guiding hand stands just behind what we are able to perceive. Jung's own experiments with astrology astonished him with their accuracy. Unable to explain these results by any scientific theory, he coined the term "synchronicity" or "meaningful coincidence." When one of these "synchronistic" events occurs, the natural reaction is amazement, awe, deep religious feelings, but most likely in the West, a simple acknowledgement of "good luck," or serendipity. The continuity of Jewish history only makes sense within an acknowledgement of synchronicity.

At each step the tiny tribe not only survives but flourishes in the face of seemingly insurmountable odds. The tribe is enslaved, it escapes to experience enlightenment at Sinai. It prospers and becomes a kingdom, only to be warned repeatedly of impending doom by its sacred technicians because it has forgotten its *raison d'êntre*. It is defeated by the Assyrian Empire, but survives when Assyria is obliterated by Babylonia. It is defeated and exiled by Babylonia, but is reassured by its sacred technicians that the exile is temporary. Its sovereignty is restored when Babylonia is obliterated by Persia. The Jewish tribe survives the

Macedonians, Ptomelies, Selucids, and Romans in the Levant, and then scatters abroad to be part of every other empire to arise in Europe, North Africa and the Middle East.

From its beginning, Jewish history is motivated by the experience of God. At every step survival is precarious. Of all the ancient tribes to be scattered from its borders, it is virtually the only one to remain. Meanwhile that history has been a most creative enterprise, spinning off Christianity and Islam, which determine the spiritual path for half the world. In the current century the will to survive in the face of greatest danger stays true to pattern, as the monsterous Holocaust is followed by the resurrection of Jewish sovereignty after a 1900 year haitus.

This pattern—empowerment by the experience of God, danger and creative survival—repeats itself, so often that it rises above itself to be transformed into something more. At each juncture, different historic forces may have made that pattern continue: sometimes they are economic, sometimes political, sometimes social or intellectual. However, taken as a whole Jewish history asks, "Is there not some meaning to the seeming coincidence that an experience of God can empower a clan for so long, through so many diverse situations?" The Jewish experience of God testifies to its own power by its very survival.

The synchronicity of Jewish history lies not in its individual events or epochs, each of which can be dissected by the historian's scalpel. The synchronicity of Jewish history is the unfolding of its totality. The sum total of Jewish history is one mammouth display of synchronicity, a terribly unlikely event of immense significance which transcends conventional, rational analysis.

Jewish "Choseness" In the Post-Technologic Age

In the Torah, God tells the descendents of Israel, "If you will obey me faithfully and keep my covenant, you shall be my treasured possession (Heb. *segula mekol ha'amim*). Indeed, all the earth is mine, but you shall be to me as a kingdom of priests and my holy nation" (EXODUS 19:5-6).

This has always been a difficult statement to take at face value: it establishes a sense of Jewish separateness and differentness. On one hand, it is narrow-minded in our global village for any one group to maintain a special claim to God's favor. Yet on the other hand, God's special favor is an archetypal experience within many of Earth's mythologies. Islam's notion of *jihad* ("holy war") is an instance where we are the object of others' experience that God has chosen them.

The Torah itself warned, "It is not because of your greatness among nations that *YHVH* sets his heart on you and chooses you, for you are insignificant among the nations" (DEUTERONO-MY 7:7). The prophets explain that being chosen is a difficult task and not one that provides benefits: "I have know you the most intimately of all the people of the earth; therefore I bring the evil you do back upon yourselves" (AMOS 3:2). In addition, the claim of Jewish "choseness" has always been an albatross, attracting and magnifying the destructive power of the Jewish archetype in others.

The synchronicity of Jewish history makes it possible to both affirm Jewish choseness and to put it into perspective. Each tribe has a natural inclination to claim a uniqueness of its own. The fact of Jewish history should make us secure enough in our own uniqueness to acknowledge the uniqueness of others.

At the same time, the 4000 year unbroken history of Jewish survival more than suggests that there is something of another dimension going on. The history of a small tribe has criss-crossed the history of half the world. It has provided leadership and creativity to virtually every field and phase of every culture in the West and Middle East. Powered by the experience of the Oneness of God and struggling against the perils of the Jewish archetype, the Jewish effect upon the world has been so essential as to indicate a Divine hand at work.

The Jewish task in the modern age is to reclaim the Jewish spiritual experiences which the technological age has hidden. That reclamation means opening to the power of Torah, understanding *halakhah*, appreciating the metaphysical significance of the land and people of Israel, looking for God through the experience of the *sephirot* and in paranormal events, meditation, and reflecting on the synchronicity of our very existence. The karma of Jewish birth imparts a tremendous potential for spiritual awareness. If the re-spiritualization of contemporary Jewish souls continues, the process will have an increasing effect upon synagogue life. A transition, which is still only a ripple, cannot help but become a major force in contemporary Jewish life. By the year 2000 of the Common Era, its power may become a torrent.

Chapter 13

Judaism — Present and Future

A Word of Caution

On the surface level, Judaism is strongly oriented towards this world and often appears to be more concerned with "how to survive in this world and make it a good place in which to live" than with "how to facilitate the experience of God."

In part, this orientation has been a reaction to external forces. For much of Jewish history, staying alive as a Jew has not been an easy matter. As a result, Judaism has developed a spirituality which demands involvement with this world in order to make it a less distressful place, and which endeavors to keep the community alive and vibrant. Ethics and culture have become so important that they sometimes appear to push spiritual experience out of the daily foreground.

Facilitating the experience of God was always the ultimate reason for living and for keeping the community alive. Amid the pressing task of everyday survival, this ultimate reason gets forgotten. A well-known Jewish metaphor demonstrates the dichotomy. The first Hebrew letter of the Torah is a *"Bet."* A *"Bet"* is shaped like a squared-off "U" turned on its side. There is an ancient explanation that says a *"Bet"* was chosen as the Torah's first letter to teach a lesson: "Just as a *"Bet"* is closed on three sides and open on one, so you must not inquire about what is above this world, what is below, what came before creation or what will occur after the world ceases to exist. You may legitimately speak about what has happened between the time the world was created until now." (*Midrash Bereshit Rabbah* 1).

Yet on the pages of this text, there are myriad metaphysical speculations about what happened before the world was created, about what dialogues and thought processes God went through before the world was created, about the structure of the seven heavens, and about what will remain when this earth is no longer.

Similarly, the Talmud warns that one should not even teach about metaphysics or ultimate reality — literally "The Essence of Creation" (*Ma'asei bereshit*) — except privately. Furthermore, one should not describe the experience of God — literally, Ezekiel's "Vision of the Chariot" (*Ma'asei merkavah*, EZEKIEL 1:4f.) — at all (B.HAGGIGAH 11b). These injunctions are also ignored on the very pages where they appear.

This discussion includes a warning that intense spiritual experiences can be dangerous. It relates the story of four of the greatest sages of the 2nd Century who devoted themselves to this quest. One went mad, one became an apostate, one died, and only one emerged transformed. The implication is that one must be well grounded on the path and proceed slowly. A familiar Jewish teaching forbids too intense spiritual work before the age of 40. However, two of the great Jewish spiritual teachers, Naḥman of Bratzlav and Isaac Luria, both died at age 39. Jung also felt that 36 was the age to begin depth analysis as only then would one be ready and have experienced enough of life and its adventures to take on the "inner life."

The way of Torah acknowledges the power of the experience of God and never forbids looking for it. However, it treats these matters cautiously. Jewish literature on how to facilitate the experience of God is either dense and obscure writing on *sephirot* and meditation, or overly concrete explications of *halakhah* and *aggadah*.

The Experience of Experience

Until the Industrial Revolution, Jewish spiritual activities were the most significant experiences of most Jews' lives. Synagogue worship, home holiday celebrations, and regular observance of the Torah's 613 Commandments provided life's central focus. Throughout the ages, when communications and entertainment were few, when travel was slow and there was relatively little one could acquire, the spiritual aspects of life had primary importance. Study of Torah, celebrations and membership in the community were the means to experiencing God. One expected to experience God as a living reality.

There is a difference between "learning about" something and "experiencing the reality" of that something. There is a distinction between reading about rollercoasters in the library, and plunging down the first hill at 90 miles per hour. In every spiritual path, religious ceremonies and rituals are the tools that facilitate the experience of God. Through prayer, meditation, song, dance, chanting, sacrifice, dietary changes, ritual, story-telling, and certain sensory experiences, the experience of God comes closer.

The experience of God is the most intense, profound, and meaningful experience a person can have. Even if you don't *believe in* God, you can have the *experience of* God. Believing in God is similar to learning about rollercoasters. It misses the best part. Often people say they don't believe in God simply because they've never had the experience.

At this time in history, Judaism-the-spiritual path has lost much of its power. If you visit your local synagogue today, you may not be overwhelmed by the intense spiritual activity going on. For many Jews, most Jewish religious activity consists of tired, empty rituals. Over the last 150 years, modern Western technology has progressively minimalized the social acceptability of religious expression. Spiritual activity must now compete with the excitement of the modern age: entertainment, consumer goods, travel, ego enhancement. Today, the vast majority of Jews are uncomfortable performing a simple spiritual act with any genuine feeling behind it.

Most modern Jews are uneasy with the ancient, unfamiliar trappings of religion. Worship of an unseen Parent-God, maintenance of sacred times, adherence to dietary regulations, and the other minutiae that Judaism demands are out of synch with the daily mindset of most Western Jews.

At the same time, most Jews have a deep feeling of "connectedness to something Jewish." Ethnicity has replaced religion as the dominant feature of Jewish civilization. The old American ideal of a "melting pot" has been replaced with the new ideal of "ratatouille," in which all the different vegetables simmer together but they retain their individual flavor. To be Jewish, Irish, Italian, Polish, Black, gay, hearing-impaired, or whatever, now gives each individual the feeling of having a unique destiny. Jews no longer try to hide their Jewish origins as they did not so long ago, or apologize for them.

The secular, ethnic activity of the Jewish community of the United States today is staggering. Millions of dollars are raised by Jews for the needs of other Jews around the world. Jews lobby our Congresspeople proudly on behalf of Israel's needs. We have walked thousands of miles to publicize the desperation of Soviet Jewry and Ethiopian Jewry. There are a flood of books published every month on Jewish cooking, historical and cultural studies. We are in the midst of what scholars will some day call "The Golden Age of American Judaism."

Judaism's greatest genius is also a great weakness. Judaism integrates a broad range of "Jewish work" into the spiritual process. The modern notion is that political action on behalf of other Jews, creation and appreciation of folk arts, production and reading of Jewish scholarship, and supporting Jewish communal institutions are important manifestations of the modern religious experience. Even more, living a basically good, honest life is regarded as exemplifying what Judaism is all about, no less than engaging in daily worship.

On one hand, this is wonderful notion. All sorts of activities serve a high spiritual purpose. However, it is too easy to be involved in such activities without pausing to feel the spiritual transformations taking place. These nonspiritual activities leave something unnameable missing. Only rarely is the experience of God facilitated through these other processes.

This situation implies that either we have outgrown our need for primitive superstitions, or else we have repressed a natural desire for intense spiritual experience at a cost to our psyches. Although a majority have "voted with their feet" for the former, an intuition towards the latter persists in a "nagging doubt" that we have lost something. Before this conundrum can be resolved, it is essential to experience what has been lost.

Stepping Back on the Path

Your first step toward re-appropriating the power of the Jewish spiritual experience is to trust your intuition when it tells you that Judaism is a spiritual path, and that you will be enriched by following it. Second, you must put aside your resistances in order to re-open yourself to spiritual experience.

It is easy to lose Judaism's forest for the trees. Judaism is made up of dozens of activities which do not always seem spiritual and which are inconvenient. Unless you investigate more deeply, Judaism's many "do's" and "don'ts" feel like components of an ethical/cultural way of life, or remnants of some unassailable, terribly romantic sense of "Tradition."

As Jews spread over the face of the earth, we have developed the strong inner sense that in addition to being a spiritual path, Judaism is a people with a common heritage, culture, values and destiny. This sense of peoplehood unites Jews and has been essential to our survival for so long. Unfortunately, when Jews become distant from the experience of God, they may mistakenly convince themselves that this "sense of peoplehood" is the primary principle of Judaism.

The word "religion" comes from the Latin: *re/ligare*. *Re*, again; *ligare*, to bind. Religion "re-binds." Therefore, opening to spiritual experience means "re-binding" to the Higher World. We live in a world nearly devoid of spirituality, a world so secularized and technologized that anything hinting at spiritual expression is an embarrassment. Our predominant Christian models of religion are either sterile Sunday morning mainline irrelevancies or raving fundamentalists of various stripes. We wish our own Orthodoxy would quietly go away.

Opening to spiritual experience means opening to the possibility that certain requirements or regulations may be essential to facilitating spiritual experience. Perhaps it means experimenting with Jewish dietary laws on a daily basis or with regular davening. Virtually every spiritual tradition has dietary regulations and daily devotions. These practices have always been responsible, in part, for the spiritual strength and transformative power of the religion.

Though we are born with strong religious impulses, most of us resist our spiritual inclinations. In a culture that has not encouraged its development, we have built up strong defenses. One must consciously resolve to penetrate through these defenses in order to re-experience these innate impulses. One must become determined to move, sing, and feel, even when it is uncomfortable.

Dynamic Tension

Finally, we must commit ourselves to entering into the dynamic tension between Judaism's exclusiveness and its openness to enrichment offered by other paths.

Judaism has always guarded the secrets of its spiritual path in what has been rightly perceived to be a hostile world. Since its origins, Judaism has had to struggle to survive, and one of our primary survival mechanisms has been distrust and rejection of competing religious systems. Canaanite, Mesopotamian, Greek, and Roman religions, Christianity and Islam have been seen as dangerous, threatening and potentially fatal to Judaism.

In Jewish religious education, children are taught stories about Jewish heroes who refused to bend their faith to their masters' will, even at the cost of their lives. Those who leave Judaism for other paths have always been regarded as traitors at best.

At the same time, Jews have always learned from the host cultures in which we've lived, and shared with them in kind. Jews learned philosophy from the Greeks, science from the Moslems; the Ba'al Shem Tov, Hasidism's founder, learned much about ecstasy from his Russian Orthodox Christian contemporaries, and Zionism would never have come into being without European nationalism.

There is a Jewish dynamic tension between "building fences around the Torah"—protecting and keeping pure what is essentially Jewish—and enchantment with and curiosity about the intellectual, cultural, or spiritual pursuits of the host cultures.

Intense spiritual experience has been lost from Jewish life. To reawaken this loss, Judaism needs an infusion of spiritual experience. That infusion is coming from wrestling with the spiritual traditions of the Far East.

There has been a fundamental change in life on this planet in recent years which Judaism has barely begun to acknowledge. The religious world in which Judaism swims is no longer restricted to the threatening Christian and Islamic systems of the previous centuries. Now the ancient spiritual paths of the Far East sit side-by-side with Judaism in every contemporary bookstore. Ashrams and dojos have taken their place in American suburbia. It is no longer possible to explain Judaism to spiritually inclined Americans without illumination from the Far Eastern traditions.

The crossroad of East and West implies a particular common

psychology—or collective unconscious—as described by Jung, who made this discovery by noting similarities among the spiritual experiences of various cultures around the world. To regain access to the power of Jewish spiritual experience, you must consider it in the light of the spiritual experiences of ancient traditions of the Far East, acknowledging where Judaism is unique, and accepting where Judaism is like other spiritual paths.

Whether or Not You Were Born into the Jewish Tribe

If you choose to travel the Jewish path, your road may be lonely. The Jewish spiritual path has always been a "minority opinion." In our day and age, the quest for intense spiritual experience in any tradition is still of interest to relatively few.

If you had the karma to be born into the Jewish tribe, you may be interested in the spiritual experiences that your tribe has evolved. This interest may not be consciously shared by your friends or family. Most Jews adopt a level of Jewish activity at an early age, based primarily on what their parents did. Now, you must be willing to go beyond that conditioning and experiment. You must decide that the pattern of Jewish experience that you've lived all your life is not your final stance. You may want to consider experiencing a total, twenty-five hour *Shabbat* rest, or changing your dietary habits. Rest assured, you will encounter resistance from your family when you announce your intentions, but remember their resistance is a mirror of your own. "Letting go of Egypt" is a long and difficult struggle.

Today we live in the Global Village, where a process of spiritual development is unfolding everywhere. The energies of the Far East, an understanding of the depths of the human psyche, together with the empowerment of women are creating changes which will indelibly stamp future Jewish spirituality. It is an exciting rollercoaster to ride.

Epilogue

A Ritual of Transformation

Expanding your spiritual experience is a long, slow process. Sometimes the process takes a large quantum leap and one feels a noticeable, dramatic change. More often, the process moves along slowly, with hardly an overwhelming moment. Only after a few months or years have passed will you be able to look back upon your experience and say, "Yes, I have grown."

However, if you have followed the text of this book and done the experiences, you have undergone a transformation. You have learned things you did not know, gained an emotional depth you did not have, and grown aware of what was hidden from you. Your ego has been purged of some of the attachments that have caused it pain. You have attained a higher, more spiritual way of being; something of your *neshamah* has struggled to be born.

The birth of a soul does not come easily. The chick must fight to break out of its shell, the salmon must jump the rapids before it can spawn, the caterpillar must die before the butterfly can emerge.

After a transformation so momentous, you deserve a ritual. A ritual of transformation is one of religion's primary *raisons d'être*. Without such a ritual, the transformation itself is incom-

plete. The ritual declares to God, to your community and to yourself, that on many levels a change of status has occurred. God
already knows, but likes to hear it; the community needs to be
told, so that it can establish new ways to relate to a long-standing
member. You already know but the ritual insures that you know
that you know.

Rituals of transformation are programmed experiences or
psychodramas designed to facilitate the experience of transformation. Jewish tradition contains a number of such rituals. You
now have the tools to appreciate this additional dimension of
Jewish spiritual experience.

The morning worship service is a mini-ritual of transformation. During the morning worship, we experience awareness of
body and soul, meditation on the Oneness of God, the *Prayer,*
study of Torah, and conclusion. Participating in each of these
components leads us through a journey. We emerge transformed
into an older, more confident and competent being who has
made it through one more day, and who is lined up at the starting blocks for yet another.

The *Shabbat* is also a ritual of transformation. It begins with
a gentle and expansive at-home celebration. This mood progresses
into midnight, when man and woman join on Earth and above.
Shabbat morning is intense davening and Torah study, which
gives way to the afternoon of yearning and visualization. Finally, *Shabbat* departs with a magical Messianic moment than steps
outside of time.

In a similar manner, the festivals of the year make up another
transformational cycle. The climax of the year and its preeminent ritual of transformation comes at *Yom Kippur*, whose high
level of spiritual awareness brings us closer to God that at any
other moment of the ritual year. By spending the day in prayer
for atonement, the past is laid to rest. We are imbued with a
sense of the passing of time and of having acquired experiences.
The last sounds of *Yom Kippur* are the *Shema* meditation, a
blast of the *shofar*, and silence. In that silence, the transition

is complete.

Finally, the life cycle itself designates certain moments for the most dramatic rituals of transformation: birth, puberty, marriage and death. At birth, the male child is branded with circumcision, acknowledging the immense power of sexuality that can be transformed to the highest purpose. (Girl-child birth rituals are still in the process of emerging.) At puberty, the child enters the realm of those enjoined to the Torah in the *Bar Miẓvah* celebration. (In this century, this ritual has been extended to girls as well, with the *Bat Miẓvah*). At marriage, young adults form the archetypal bond of male and female sides of a single being. At death, the mourners accompany the deceased as far as they can, to the edge of the next world, before returning to this world. Each of these ceremonies celebrates a change from one stage of life's way to another.

Experience 31

Ritual of Transformation

1) Prepare a tape of the text below (#3), or have someone with you to read it.

2) Find a quiet place and relax. Once you are totally relaxed and your eyes have closed, listen to the following:

3) Imagine yourself in a meadow. It is a meadow that is both familiar and new. See the grass and the trees. Hear its sounds. Feel the warmth of the day on your body. See before you a mountain. Notice that there is a path that goes all the way to the top...and that it is a well travelled path...that many other have been on that path before you.

Begin to walk up the mountain. You find that you are able to climb easily. Be aware of what your thoughts are, what you see and hear, what you are feeling. Now notice that you are be-

ginning to reach the top of this mountain. The summit is near.
As you reach the top, look around. From the top you can see
for many miles. Pay attention to what you see. What is your perspective from here? What is it like to be standing here?

Look up toward the sun. Its rays of light radiate in all directions. Notice that one single ray of light is coming directly towards
you. This ray touches the ground at your feet. Notice that the
ray appears to be substantial. It is strong enough for you to walk
on. Take a step and stand on it. It supports you. Walk along
that ray of light, along that sunbeam towards the sun. It feels
strong beneath your feet. As you walk there is a pleasant breeze
blowing in your face.

As you walk up this sunbeam, experience the light of the sun
within you. It is clearing your vision, clearing your mind. Feel
this new clarity within you. As you walk with this new clarity,
you notice around you there are many others, also walking along
their own sunbeams toward the sun. You recognized some of
the people from your current life, some from your past life, and
some you will know in the future.

As you continue to climb, you begin to experience the quality of joy, the joy of this climb, the joy of being on your own
path, the joy of climbing along with others, the joy of moving
in the light of the sun.

Soon you find that your path and the other paths begin to
merge together into one broad road towards the sun. You are
all on the same path, some ahead of you, some beside you and
others behind. You are travelling together towards the sun. You
turn and notice that some people are back at the base of the
mountain, just beginning to embark on their journey. Some are
about to step onto their own sunbeam. You experience love and
compassion for those who are behind you. You feel that you want
to help them. You are aware that as you travel you help prepare
the path for the ones who will come after you.

As you look ahead, see those who are helping you. They are
preparing the way for you. You recognize that they are doing

this because of their love and compassion for those behind them. You realize that there is love and compassion flowing from the sun to everyone on these paths, and on the one path as everyone climbs together.

As you continue moving closer to the sun, you experience its light, and joy and love and compassion. You begin to experience the power that comes from the sun, and that power gives you power to help others, power to overcome obstacles, power to allow yourself to be helped by others.

You are getting close to the sun, and the experience of the light. The joy and love and compassion and power begin to come together, closer and closer, until it is almost impossible to distinguish them separately. The energies of each of them are becoming one energy. You notice other qualities are emerging as well: beauty, trust, order, wisdom...and all of these are beginning to merge into one, one energy from that one great source.

As you enter the sun, you experience that merging. Other things may happen as you experience the merging. Allow them. You may hear sounds, or experience other qualities coming together. Move toward the center of the sun. Allow yourself to experience what it is like to stand at the center of the sun. From the center you can look out, down that broad ray of light along which people are travelling.

See the connection between you and the earth. Ask yourself, "Why would I want to go back down?" Let the answer emerge from within you. See the people travelling on that path. You can see them as points of light. Some are still on their way to the mountain, some are on the mountain, some are on their individual beams of light, still others are on the great path.

Begin now to move away from the center of the sun and out of the sun and back down the path, slowly. As you do, experience that there is a golden thread of energy at the top of your head connected to the center of the sun. Notice that this thread is there as you move down the path. It is a connection between you and the sun and it links you together.

As you move down the path, you pass others who are going up toward the sun. You see that there are others moving down the path. As you travel back down, the golden thread of energy still connects you to the sun and it keeps bringing you that energy that you experienced at the center of the sun. You keep that with you as you move back onto the mountain.

As you arrive at the top of the mountain, pause for a moment and be aware of the energy that you bring from the sun. Look out once again and be aware of what you see, of what you know. Move down the mountain, still connected by the golden thread to that miraculous source of energy. Pause for a moment to be in touch with that energy and be in touch with the knowing that comes with it. Remember that any time you forget or you lose the energy or the knowing, you can refocus your attention on that thread, and you can re-connect yourself to the sun.

Now, as I count to five, you are going to bring yourself back into the room, where you will remember every detail of what occurred on your trip, especially the fact that the golden thread is still there. You will awaken feeling very refreshed.

Glossary

Glossary of Hebrew, Jungian and Eastern terms. [Terms which appear only once and are defined where used are not included]

AHYH—a name of God. It stands for the Hebrew letters which form the word, "I am" or "I will be." At the Burning Bush, Moses asks God for a name and God replies, "*AHYH* Asher *AHYH*," "I am what I am" or "I will be what I will be." See "*YHVH*".

Aggadah—(Heb.) Torah's mythologizing process: finding life's meaning by probing the meaning of Torah's text. Literally, "The telling." Approximately synonymous with "Midrash."

Anima/Animus—Jung's terms to describe a man's psychic construct of the ideal woman within (anima) or the woman's equivalent male within (animus). The assimilation of the energy of the anima/animus is an essential part of the process of individuation.

Archetype—Jung's term for the recurring patterns that emerge from the psyche throughout various ages and cultures. The idealized pictures of human categories. See "collective unconscious."

BCE—"Before Common Era"—a more scientific and universal designation for "BC," Before Christ.

CE—"Common Era,"—equivalent to AD. See "BCE".

213

Chakra—The seven centers of energy in the human body, where a variety of phenomena, particularly spiritual events are experienced.

Collective unconscious—Jung's term for that part of the human unconscious which is innate and not dependent upon individual experience for its contents. It is the ground out of which the archetypes arise.

Conservative Judaism— see "Jewish Movements, Contemporary"

Dharma—Fundamental Buddhist term meaning universal Law, phenomena, Truth, Buddhist doctrine, the teachings of the Buddha.

Erez Yisrael—(Heb.) The Land of Israel

Gemara—(Aramaic) The encyclopedic commentary on the Mishna. Literally, "Conclusions." See "Talmud".

HaKadosh Barukh Hu—(Heb.) A name for God. Usually, denoting the masculine side of God, counterbalancing God's feminine side which is called "Shekhinah." Literally, "The Holy Blessed One," or "The Holy One, Blessed Be He."

Halakhah—(Heb.) The specific actions demanded by the Way of Torah. Literally, "The Way."

Hasidic movement, or Hasidism— A movement for Jewish spiritual renewal which flourished in 18th century Eastern Europe. Hasidism is characterized by the predominant role of the Rebbe or Spiritual Master of the community. Hasidic communities are still to be found in several American cities and in Israel.

Havdalah—(Heb.) The ceremony which marks the conclusion of Shabbat. Literally, "separation."

Individuation—Jung's term for the overall process of spiritual growth.

Jewish Movements, Contemporary—The contemporary Jewish world is divided in three major movements, each with its own organizational structure and its own approach to spirituality. Reform takes the most liberal approach, Orthodoxy the most fundamental, Conservative the center of the road.

Karma—In Buddhism and Hinduism, the universal laws of cause and effect that determine all things.

Kashrut—(Heb.) The laws of "kosher-ness." See "Kosher".

Kavannah—(Heb.) The intensity or intention within an individual who performs a spiritual act. Literally, "intention".

Kedushah—(Heb.) "Holiness", numinosity, other-ness, different-ness.

Ketuvim—(Heb.) "Writings." The third and final subdivision of the Hebrew Bible, including the books of Psalms, Proverbs, Job and others. See "Tanakh".

Kiddush—(Heb.) A prayer recited over wine that begins Shabbat. Literally, "Sanctification", or "declaring it 'Kodesh'".

Kodesh—(Heb.) Holy, numinous, other, unique; noun form of "Kedushah".

Kundalini—(Sanskrit) Human energy which is concentrated in the Chakras. Spiritual activity activates kundalini and raises it from the lower to the higher Chakras. Literally, "Serpent power."

Luria's circle—Group of intense spiritual figures who studied together with Rabbi Isaac Luria, in the 16th century Israeli town of Safad. Articulated the predominant patterns of Jewish spiritual thought since.

Mashiah—(Heb.) "The Anointed One," or "Messiah," for which Jewish tradition still waits in anticipation. See "Messiah".

Messiah—The individual or movement or force which will restore both the physical and spiritual destiny of the Jewish tribe. See "Mashiah".

Midrash—The process of probing the Torah's text to find its true meaning. Literally, "Probing." See "aggadah".

Mishpat—(Heb.) "Justice". One of the essential ideals and goals of Halakhah.

Mizvot (pl.)/ Mizvah (sing.)—The 613 "Commandments" of the Torah which make up the particulars of Halakhah.

Mozi—Prayer recited over bread. Literally, "Who brings forth," as it praises God "Who brings forth bread from the earth."

Nefesh—(Heb.) The first level of the human psyche, consisting of animal, emotional and rational components. See "*ru-aḥ*" and "*neshamah*".

Neshamah—(Heb.) The third level of the human psyche, consisting of the spiritual inclinations. See "*nefesh*" and "*ru-aḥ*."

Nevi'im—(Heb.) The Prophets who explicated Torah from Moses' death for about 800 years, or the books which bear their names and which form the second of three parts of the Hebrew Bible. See "*Tanakh.*"

Orthodox Judaism—see "Jewish Movements, Contemporary"

Olam Ha-ba—(Heb.) "The World to Come." Refers to a distinct epoch in the future: either the time of the Messiah or to an afterlife.

Pesaḥ—(Heb.) Passover. The festival which commemorates the Exodus from Egypt.

Rebbe—See "Hasidic movement".

Reform Judaism—see "Jewish Movements, Contemporary"

Ru-aḥ—(Heb.) The second of three levels of the human psyche, consisting of the realm of discrimination and ethical decision-making.

Sekhar ve-onesh—(Heb.) The Jewish equivalent of karma, the universal law of cause and effect. Literally, "Reward and punishment".

Sephirot (pl.)/ *sephira* (sing.)—(Heb.) The Jewish equivalent of Chakras, the energy centers of the body where spiritual experience is perceived. Also the attributes or emanations of God which humans are capable of experiencing.

Shabbat—(Heb.) The Sabbath. Saturday on the contemporary

calendar. One day in seven devoted solely to spiritual activity.

Shadow—Jung's terms for those aspects of the personality which are deemed unacceptable and repressed into the unconscious. They form a more or less automonous splinter personality which projects its own contents onto others. Bringing the shadow to consciousness is an essential part of the process of Individuation.

Shekhinah—(Heb.) a name of God, denoting God's immanence or ready availability and the feminine aspects of God. See "HaKadosh Barukh Hu."

Shema—(Heb.) The meditation on the Oneness of God, comprising a central element in Jewish liturgy. Literally, "Listen!"

Siddur—(Heb.) Hebrew prayerbook. Literally, "order," as the services follow a prescribed order.

Sidrah—(Aramaic) One of the weekly sections of the Torah in the Synagogue's annual Torah-reading cycle. Literally, "order."

Synchronicity—Jung's term for "meaningful coincidence."

Taharah—(Heb.) The state of ritual purity. Opposite of "Tamei."

Talmud—The encyclopedic commentary on the Torah, committed to writing c.600 CE. Comprised of the *Mishnah* and the *Gemara*.

Tamei—(Heb.) One who is in state of Tumah.

Tanakh—(Heb.) Jewish name for the Hebrew Bible. Acronym of its three parts, Torah, Nevi'im, and Ketuvim.

Tefillah—(Heb.) Prayer in general or specifically "The Prayer" of the daily worship services.

Tikkun Olam—(Heb.) Mending the world. Performance of spiritual actions to improve the overall condition of the Planet.

Tumah—(Heb.) Ritual impurity attained through intimate awareness of the mystery of life and death, specifically through a woman's menstrual period or contact with a corpse. Opposite of "Taharah."

yang—see yin/yang

YHVH—(Heb.) Most powerful name of God whose correct pronounciation has been lost for 2000 years. Linked etymologically to AHYH, "I am."

yin/yang—The harmonious opposite forces which are everpresent in nature. *Yin* is earth, receptive, feminine energy; *yang* is sky, active, masculine energy.

Yom Kippur—(Heb.) The Day of Atonement, most awesome day of the Jewish year, spent in prayer, fasting, and self-scrutiny.

Zedek—"Rightness." One of the essential ideals that halakhah strives to promote.

Bibliography

Arguelles, Jose and Miriam. *Mandala*. Berkely, CA: Shambhala 1972.

Aron, Milton. *Ideas and Ideals of Hassidim*. Secaucus, NJ: Citadel Press 1969.

Ashlag, Yehuda. *Sefer HaZohar im Perush HaSulam* (Heb.). Jerusalem: no publisher listed 1965.

Ashlag, Yehuda. *Ten Luminous Emanations from Rabbi Isaac Luria* (2 Vols). Jerusalem: Research Centre for Kabbalah 1973.

Assagioli, Roberto. *Act of Will, The*. Middlesex, Eng: Penguin Books 1973.

Assagioli, Roberto. *Psychosynthesis: A Manual of Principles and Techniques*. New York: Viking Press 1971.

Bachya ben Joseph ibn Paquda. *Hovot HaLevavot/Duties of the Heart* (Heb/Eng, 2 vols). Jerusalem: Boys Town Jerusalem Publishers 1965.

Bahir, The, Aryeh Kaplan, transl. York Beach, Maine: Samuel Weiser. 1979.

Bazak, Jacob. *Judaism and Psychical Phenomena*. New York: Garrett Publications 1972.

Ben-Amos, Dan & Mintz, J. *In Praise of the Baal Shem Tov*. Bloomington, IN: Indiana Univ Pr. 1970.

Bension, Ariel. *The Zohar in Moslem and Christian Spain*. New York: Hermon Press 1932.

Berg, Philip. *Entrance to the Zohar, An*. Jerusalem: Research Centre for Kabbalah 1974.

Berg, Philip. *The Wheels of the Soul*. Jerusalem: Research Centre of Kabbalah 1984.

Bhagavad Gita, The. Transl. by Franklin Edgerton. New York: Harper & Rowe. 1944.

Blank, William. "A Jewish View of Reincarnation," *Four Worlds Journal*, Vol 2, No 3, Spring 1985, p. 13.

Blank, William. "Domesticating Peak Experiences". *Body Mind Spirit*, Issue No. 35, Vol 8, No 5, October, 1989, p. 24.

Blank, William. "The Royal Road: A Beginning Lesson". *Meditation* Vol 4, No 1, Winter 1988/89, p. 24.

Blank, William. "Torah and Tantra". *Body Mind Spirit,* Issue No. 33, Vol 8, No 3, June, 1989, p. 58.

Blank, William. "Why a Reform Rabbi Davens in a Conservative Shul". *Jounal of Reform Judaism*, Vol 36 No 1, Winter 1989, p 1.

Blumenthal, David. *Understanding Jewish Mysticism* (2 vols). New York: Ktav 1978, 1982.

Bohm, David. *Quantum Theory and Beyond*. Cambridge: Cambridge Univ Press 1971.

Bokser, Ben Zion. *Jewish Mystical Tradition, The*. New York: Pilgrim Press. 1981.

Bokser, Ben Zion, Editor. *The Essential Writings of Abraham Isaac Kook*. Amity, New York: Amity House 1988.

Borowitz, Eugene. *The Mask Jews Wear*. Port Washington, NY: Sh'ma 1973.

Bultmann, Rudolf. *Jesus Christ and Mythology*. New York: Charles Scribner's Sons 1958.

Bultmann, Rudolf. *Theology of the New Testament*. New York: Charles Scribner's Sons 1951, 1958.

Byrd, R., "Positive Therapeutic Effects of Intercessory Prayer in a Coronary Care Unit Population," *Southern Medical Journal*, Vol 81, No 7, p. 826.

Campbell, Joseph. *Masks of God, The* (4 vols). Middlesex, GB: Penguin 1964.

Campbell, Joseph. *Myths to Live By*. New York: Bantam 1972.

Campbell, Joseph with Moyers, Bill. *Power of Myth, The*. New York: Doubleday 1988.

Capra, Fritjof. *The Tao of Physics*. Boulder, CO: Shambhala 1975.

Chia, Mantak & Chia, Maneeway. *Cultivating Female Sexual Energy: Healing Love Through the Tao*. Huntington, NY: Healing Tao Books 1986.

Chia, Mantak & Winn, Michael. *Taoist Secrets of Love: Cultivating Male Sexual Energy*. New York: Aurora Press 1984.

Cohen, Martin Samuel. *The Shi'ur Qomah: Liturgy and Theurgy in Pre-Kabbalistic Jewish Mysticism*. Lanham, NY: University Press of America 1983.

Coxhead, Nona. *The Relevance of Bliss: a Contemporary Exploration of Mystic Experience*. New York: St Martin's Press 1985.

Dawidowicz, Lucy. *The Holocaust and the Historians*. Cambridge, MA: Harvard Univ Pr. 1981.

Dawidowicz, Lucy. *War Against the Jews, 1933-1945, The*. New York: Holt Rinehart and Winston 1975.

Deikeman, Arthur J. *The Observing Self: Mysicism and Psychotherapy*. Boston: Beacon Press 1982.

Donin, Hayim Halevy. *To Pray As A Jew: A Guide to the Prayer Book and the Synagogue Service*. New York: Basic Books 1980.

Douglas, Nik and Slinger, Penny. *Sexual Secrets: The Alchemy of Ecstasy*. New York: Destiny Books 1979.

Dresner, Samuel. *The World of a Hasidic Master: Levi Yitzhak of Berditchev*. New York: Shapolsky Pub. 1986.

Dresner, Samuel. *Zaddik, The: The Doctrine of the Zaddik According to the Writings of Rabbi Yaakov Yosef of Polony*. New York: Schocken 1960.

Early Kabbalah, The. Dan, Joseph, editor. New York: Paulist Press 1986.

Eastcott, Michal. *The Silent Path: An Introduction to Meditation*. London: Rider & Co. 1969.

Eisler, Riane. *The Chalice and the Blade*. San Francisco: Harper & Row 1987.

Eliade, Mircea. *Myth and Reality*. New York: Harper Torch 1963.

Eliade, Mircea. *Patterns in Comparative Religion*. New York: Meridian World 1963.

Eliade, Mircea. *Yoga, Immortality and Freedom*. Princeton, NJ: Bollingen/Princeton University Press 1958.

Encyclopedia Judaica (16 Vols). Jerusalem: Keter 1972.

Evans-Wentz, W.Y. *Tibetan Book of the Dead, The*. London: Oxford University Press 1960.

Evans-Wentz, W.Y. *Tibetan Yoga and Secret Doctrines*. London: Oxford University Press 1958.

Fackenheim, Emil. *Quest for Past and Future: Essays in Jewish Theology*. Bloomington, IN: Indiana University Press 1968.

Feldenkrais, Moshe. *Awareness Through Movement*. New York: Harper & Row 1972.

Ferruci, Peiro. *What We May Be: Techniques for Psychological and Spiritual Growth*. Los Angeles: JP Tarcher 1982.

Flannery, Edward. *The Anguish of the Jews: Twenty-three Centuries of Anti-Semitism,* New York: Macmillan 1965.

Fleer, Gedaliah. *Rabbi Nachman's Foundation*. New York: Ohr MiBreslov 1976.

Fleischner, Eva, Editor. *Auschwitz: Beginning of a New Era?*. New York: Ktav 1977.

Freud, Sigmund. *Future of an Illusion, The*. New York: Vintage 1927.

Freud, Sigmund. *Moses and Monotheism*. New York: Vintage 1939.

Friedman, Irving. *Book of Creation: Sepher Yetzirah*, New York: Samuel Weiser, Inc. 1977.

Friedman, Philip. *Roads to Extiction: Essays on the Holocaust*. Philadelphia: Jewish Publication Society 1980.

Garrison, Omar. *Tantra: The Yoga of Sex*. New York: Julian Press 1983.

Ginsburg, Elliot. *The Sabbath in the Classical Kabbalah*. Albany, NY: State University of NY Press 1989.

Ginzberg, Louis. *The Legends of the Jews* (7 vols). Philadelphia: Jewish Publication Society 1968.

Gonen, Jay. *A Psychohistory of Zionism*. New York: New American Library 1975.

Gottlieb, Feeman. *The Lamp of God: A Jewish Book of Light*. Northvale, NJ: Jason Aronson Inc. 1989.

Graves, R. and Patai, R. *Hebrew Myths: the Book of Genesis*. New York: McGraw-Hill 1966.

Graves, Robert. *The White Goddess*. New York: Farrar, Straus and Giroux 1948.

Green, Alan S. *Sex, God and the Sabbath: The Mystery of Jewish Marriage*. Cleveland, OH: Temple Emanu El 1979.

Green, Arthur. *Tormented Master: A Life of Rabbi Nahman of Bratslav*. University, AL: Univ of Alabama Press 1979.

Green, A & Holtz, B. *Your Word is Fire: The Hasidic Masters on Contemplative Prayer*. New York: Paulist Press 1977.

Grof, Stanislav, Editor. *Ancient Wisdom and Modern Science*. Albany, NY: State University of New York Press 1984.

Grosser, Paul & Halperin, Edwin. *Anti-Semitism; The Causes and Effects of a Prejudice*. Seacaucus, NJ: Citadel Press 1979.

Hall, James A. *Jungian Dream Interpretation: A Handbook of Theory and Practice*. Toronto, Ont: Inner City Books 1983.

Hannah, Barbara. *Encounters with the Soul: Active Imagination as Developed by CG Jung*. Boston: Sigo Press 1981.

Haymond, Robert. "On Carl Gustav Jung: Psycho-social Basis of Morality During the Nazi Era". *Journal of Psychology and Judaism*, Vol 6 No 2, Spring/Summer 1982, p. 81.

Head, Joseph and Cranston, S.L., Editors. *Reincarnation: the Phoenix Fire Mystery*. New York: Julian Press 1977.

Heifetz, Harold, editor. *Zen and Hasidism*. Wheaton, IL: Quest 1978

Heinemann, Benno. *The Maggid of Dubno and his Parables*. New York: Feldheim 1978.

Herrigel, Eugen. *Zen in the Art of Archery*. New York: Vintage Books 1971.

Heschel, Abraham Joshua. *God in Search of Man: a Philosophy of Judaism*. Philadelphia: Jewish Publication Society 1959.

Heschel, Abraham Joshua. *Israel: the Echo of an Eternity*. New York: Farrar, Straus and Giroux 1969.

Heschel, Abraham J. *The Circle of the Baal Shem Tov*. Chicago: Chicago Univ Press 1985.

Heschel, Abraham Joshua. *The Sabbath: its Meaning for Modern Man*. New York: Farrar, Straus and Giroux 1951.

Hilberg, Raul. *The Destruction of the European Jews*. New York: Franklin Watts 1973.

Hillman, James. *Anima: An Anatomy of a Personified Notion*. Dallas, TX: Spring Publications 1985.

Hoffman, Lawrence. *Beyond the Text: A Holistic Approach to Liturgy*. Bloominton Indiana: Indiana University Press 1989.

Hoffman, Edward. *The Heavenly Ladder: The Jewish Guide to Inner Growth*. San Francisco: Harper & Row 1985.

Hoffman, Edward. *The Way of Splendor: Jewish Mysticism and Modern Psychology*. Boulder, CO: Shambhala 1981.

Holtz, Barry, editor. *Back to the Sources: Reading the Classic Jewish Texts*. New York: Summit Books 1984.

Houston, Jean. *The Search for the Beloved*. Los Angeles: J P Tarcher 1987.

Houston, Jean. *The Possible Human*. Los Angeles: J P Tarcher 1982.

Howell, Alice. *Jungian Symbolism in Astrology*. Wheaton, IL: Quest Books 1987.

I Ching. Edited by Raymond Van Over. New York: New American Library. 1971.

Idel, Moshe. *Studies in Ecstatic Kabbalah*. Albany, NY: State University of New York 1988.

Idel, Moshe. *The Mystical Experience in Abraham Abulafia* Albany, NY: State University of New York Press 1988.

Israel Baal Shem Tov. *The Baal Shem Tov on Pirkey Avoth*. Jerusalem: Jerusalem Academy Publication 1974.

Jacobs, Louis. *Hasidic Thought*. New York: Behrman House 1976.

Jacobs, Louis. *Hasidic Prayer*. Philadelphia: Jewish Pub Society 1973.

Jacobs, Louis. *Jewish Mystical Testimonies*. New York: Schocken Books 1976.

Jacobs, Louis. *On Ecstacy: A Tract by Dobh Baer of Lubavitch*. Chappaqua, NY: Rossel Books 1963.

Jacobs, Louis. *What Does Judaism Say About...?* New York: Quadrangle/New York Times 1973.

James, William. *The Varieties of Religious Experience*. New York: Mentor 1958.

Janowitz, Naomi. *The Poetics of Ascent: Theories of Language in a Rabbinic Ascent Text*. Albany, NY: State University of NY Press 1989.

Jayanti, Amber. *Living the Tarot: Applying an Ancient Oracle to the Challenges of Modern Life*. North Hollywood, CA: Newcastle Publishing Co. 1988.

Johnson, Robert. *We: Understanding the Psychology of Romantic Love*. San Francisco: Harper & Row 1983.

Jung, Carl Gustav. *Analytical Psychology: Its Theory and Practice*. New York: Pantheon/Random House 1968.

Jung, Carl Gustav. *Answer to Job*. Princeton, NJ: Princeton/Bollingen 1973.

Jung, Carl Gustav. *Dreams*. Princeton, NJ: Princeton/Bollingen 1974.

Jung, Carl G. *Man and His Symbols*. Garden City, NJ: Doubleday & Co. 1964.

Jung, Carl Gustav. *Mandala Symbolism*. Princeton, NJ: Princeton/Bollingen 1972.

Jung, Carl Gustav. *Memories, Dreams and Reflections*. New York: Vintage/Random House 1963.

Jung, Carl Gustav. *Modern Man in Search of a Soul*. New York: Harvest/Harcourt Brace Jovanovich 1933.

Jung, Carl Gustav. *Psyche and Symbol*. Garden City, NJ: Doubleday/Anchor 1958.

Jung, Carl Gustav. *Psychological Types*. Princeton, NJ: Princeton/Bollingen 1971.

Jung, Carl Gustav. *Psychology and Religion*. New Haven, CN: Yale Univ Press 1938.

Jung, Carl Gustav. *Synchronicity*. Princeton, NJ: Princeton/Bollingen 1973.

Jung, Carl Gustav. *Two Essays on Analytical Psychology*. Princeton, NJ: Princeton/Bollingen 1972.

Kaplan, Aryeh. *Chasidic Masters: Their Teachings*. New York: Maznaim 1984.

Kaplan, Aryeh. *Jewish Meditation: A Practical Guide*. New York: Schocken 1985.

Kaplan, Aryeh. *Light Beyond, The: Adventures in Hassidic Thought*. New York: Maznaim 1981.

Kaplan, Aryeh. *Meditation and Kabbalah*. York Beach, Maine: Samuel Weiser 1982.

Kaplan, Aryeh. *Meditation and the Bible*. York Beach, Maine: S. Weiser 1978

Kaplan, Aryeh. *Rabbi Nachman: Outpouring of the Soul*. Jerusalem: Yeshiva Chasidei Breslov 1980.

Kapleau, Philip. *The Three Pillars of Zen*. Boston: Beacon Press 1965.

Karo, Joseph. *Shulhan Arukh* (Heb. "The Table Setting"). Jerusalem: High College of A. Iger 1966.

Kirsch, James. "Carl Gustav Jung and the Jews: the Real Story" *Journal of Psychology and Judaism*, Vol 6 No 2, Spring/Summer 1982, p. 113.

Klein, Isaac. *A Guide to Jewish Religious Practice*. New York: Jewish Theological Seminary 1979.

Kluger, Rivkah S. *Psyche and Bible*. Zurich: Spring Publications 1974.

Kook, Abraham Isaac. *The Lights of Repentence*. New York: Yeshiva University Press 1978.

Kushner, Lawrence. *Honey from the Rock: Visions of Jewish Mystical Renewal*. San Francisco: Harper & Row 1977.

Kushner, Lawrence. *River of Light: Spirituality, Judaism, and the Evolution of Consciousness*. San Francisco: Harper & Row 1981.

LaBerge, Stephen. *Lucid Dreaming*. New York: Ballantine Books 1985.

Lankton, S and Lankton, C. *The Answer Within: A Clinical Framework of Eriksonian Hypnotherapy*. New York: Brunner/Mazel 1983.

Larousse Encyclopedia of Mythology. New York: Prometheus Press 1960.

Leadbeater, C.W. *The Chakras*. Wheaton, Ill: Theosophical Publishing House 1972.

Legett, Trevor. *Zen and the Ways*. Boulder: Shambhala 1978.

Levine, Stephen. *A Gradual Awakening*. Garden City, NY: Anchor/Doubleday 1979.

Littell, Franklin. *The Crucifixion of the Jews,*. New York: Harper & Row 1975.

Locks, Gutman. *The Spice of Torah - Gematria*. New York: Judaica Press 1985.

Lodo, Venerable Lama. *Bardo Teachings: The Way of Death and Rebirth*. San Francisco, KDK Publications. 1982

Luzzato, Moses. *General Principles of the Kabbalah*. Jerusalem: Research Center for Kabbalah 1970.

Maimonides, Moses. *The Guide of the Perplexed*, S. Pines, Transl. Chicago: University of Chicago Press 1963.

Maimonides, Moses. *Commandments, The*. London: Soncino 1967.

Maimonides, Moses. *Moreh Nevukhim* (Heb. "The Guide to the Perplexed"). Jerusalem: no publisher 1960.

Maritain, Jacques. *Approaches to God*. New York: Macmillan 1954.

Maslow, Abraham. *Farther Reaches of Human Nature, The*. New York: Viking Press 1971.

Maslow, Abraham. *Religions, Values, and Peak-Experiences*. New York: Viking Press 1970.

Masters, Robert and Houston, Jean. *Mind Games: a Guide to Inner Space*. New York: Delta 1974.

McClain, Florence. *A Practical Guide to Past Life Regression*. St. Paul, MN: LLewellyn Publicatons 1986.

McGiffert, Arthur C. *A History of Christian Thought* (2 vols). New York: Charles Scribner's Sons 1932.

McGill, Ormond. *Hypnotism and Mysticism of India*. Los Angles: Westwood Pub. 1979.

Meltzer, David. *Secret Garden, The: An Anthology in the Kabbalah*. New York: Seabury Press 1976.

Menahem Nahum of Chernobyl. *Upright Practices, The Light of the Eyes*. New York: Paulist Press 1982.

Mencken, H.L. *Treatise on the Gods*. New York: Vintage/Random House 1963.

Merton, Thomas. *The New Man*. New York: Mentor/Omega 1961.

Metzner, Ralph. *Maps of Consciousness*. New York: Macmillan 1971.

Midrash Rabbah (12 Vols., Eng. transl.). London: Soncino 1939.

Midrash Rabbah im Kol HaMefarshim (Heb.) (Midrash Rabbah with all Commentaries). Vilna Edition, Jerusalem 1961.

Mindell, Arnold. *Dreambody*. Boston: Sigo Press 1982.

Mishnah, The, H. Danby, transl. Oxford: Oxford Univ Press 1933.

Mishra, Rammurti S. *Yoga Sutras: The Textbook of Yoga Psychology*. Garden City, NY: Anchor/Doubleday 1973.

Motoyama, Hiroshi. *Theories of the Chakras: Bridge to Higher Consciousness*. Wheaton, Ill: Theosophical Publishing House 1981.

Nahman of Bratlav. *The Tales*. New York: Paulist Press 1978.

Neumann, Erich. *The Origins and History of Consciousness*. Princeton, NJ: Bollingen/Princeton Univ Press 1954.

Nhat Hanh, Thich. *The Miracle of Mindfulness!* Boston: Beacon Press. 1975, 1976.

Nichols, Sallie. *Jung and Tarot: an Archetypal Journey*. York Beach, Maine: S. Weiser, Inc. 1980.

Otto, Rudolph. *The Idea of the Holy*. New York: Oxford Univ Press 1958.

Parkes, James. *The Conflict of the Church and the Synagogue: A Study in the Origins of Antisemitism*. Philadelphia: Jewish Publication Society 1961.

Patai, Raphael. *Hebrew Goddess, The*. New York: Ktav 1967.

Patai, Raphael. *Jewish Mind, The*. New York: Charles Scribner's Sons 1977.

Patai, Raphael. *The Messiah Texts*. New York: Avon 1979.

Pawlikowski, John. *Catechetics and Prejudice*. 1973.

Peat, F. David. *Synchronicity: The Bridge Between Matter and Mind*. New York: Bantam New Age 1987.

Poliakov, Leon. *History of Anti-Semitism from the Time of Christ to the Court Jews, The*. New York: Schocken 1974.

Poncé, Charles. *Kabbalah: an Introduction and Illumination for the World Today*. San Francisco: Straight Arrow Books 1973

Primram, Karl. *The Languages of the Brain*. Englewood Cliffs, NJ: Prentice Hall 1971.

Ram Dass. *Jouney of Awakening: A Meditator's Guidebook*. New York: Bantam 1978.

Ram Dass. *Only Dance There Is, The*. Garden City, NJ: Anchor/Doubleday 1974.

Reik, Theodor. *Ritual: Pscyho-Analytic Studies*. New York: International Universities Press, 1946.

Rollins, Wayne. *Jung and the Bible*. Atlanta, GA: John Knox Press 1983.

Rosenberg, Roy. *The Anatomy of God*. New York: Ktav 1973.

Rothenberg, Jerome. *Technicians of the Sacred*. Garden City, NY: Anchor/Doubleday 1969.

Ruether, Rosemary. *Faith and Fratricide: The Theological Roots of Anti-Semitism*. 1974.

Safed Spirituality: Rules of Mystical Piety, The Beginning of Wisdom. Fine, L, Transl. New York: Paulist Press 1984.

Sandmel, Samuel. *Anti-Semitism in the New Testament*. Philadelphia: Fortress Press 1978.

Sarachek, Joseph. *The Doctrine of the Messiah in Medieval Jewish Literature*. New York: Hermon Press 1968.

Saraswati, S and Avinasha, B. *Jewel in the Lotus: the Sexual Path to Higher Consciousness*. San Francisco: Kriya Jyoti Tantra Society 1987.

Sarna, Nahum. *Understanding Genesis: The Heritage of Biblical Israel*. New York: Schocken 1970.

Schachter, Zalman and Hoffman, Edward. *Sparks of Light: Counseling in the Hasidic Tradition*. Boulder, CO: Shambala 1983.

Schachter-Shalomi, Zalman. *The First Step: A Guide for the New Jewish Spirit*. Toronto: Bantam 1983.

Schacter, Zalman. *Fragments of a Future Scroll: Hassidism for the Aquarian Age*. Germantown, PA: Leaves of Grass Press 1975.

Schaya, Leo. *The Universal Meaning of the Kabbalah*. Baltimore, MD: Penguin 1972.

Schneerson, Menachem. *On the Essence of Chassidus.* Brooklyn, NY: Kehot Pub Soc. 1086.

Schneur Zalman of Liady. *Likutei Amarim - Tanya.* London: Kehot Publication Society 1973.

Scholem, Gershom. *Jewish Gnosticism, Merkabah Mysticism and Talmudic Tradition.* New York: Jewish Theologic Seminary Press 1965.

Scholem, Gershom. *Kabbalah.* New York: Quadrangle/New York Times Book Co. 1974.

Scholem, Gershom. *Major Trends in Jewish Mysticism.* New York: Schocken Books 1961.

Scholem, Gershom. *Messianic Idea in Judaism and Other Essays on Jewish Spirituality, The.* New York: Schocken 1974.

Scholem, Gershom. *On the Kabbalah and Its Symbolism.* New York: Schocken 1969.

Scholem, Gershom. *Shabbatai Sevi: The Mystical Messiah.* Princeton, NJ: Princeton/Bollingen 1973.

Schrire, T. *Hebrew Magic Amulets: The Deciferment and Interpretation.* New York: Behrman House 1966.

Secret of the Golden Flower, The: A Chinese Book of Life. Transl by Richard Wilhelm, Commentary by CG Jung. New York: Harcourt, Brace & World, Inc. 1962.

Sefer HaZohar (Heb. The Zohar, 3 vols). Jerusalem: Musad HaRav Kook 1984.

Sefer Yezirah (Heb.). Jerusalem: Lewin Epstein 1965.

Siegel, Bernie. *Love, Medicine and Miracles.* New York: Harper & Row 1986.

Siegle, R., Strassfeld, M, and Strassfeld, S. *The (First) Jewish Catalog.* Philadelphia: Jewish Publication Society 1973.

Silberman, Charles. *A Certain People: American Jews and their Lives Today.* New York: Summit Books 1984.

Silver, Abba Hillel. *Where Judaism Differed: an Inquiry into the Distinctiveness of Judaism.* New York: Macmillan 1956.

Singer, June. *Androgyny.* Garden City, NJ: Anchor/Doubleday 1977.

Singer, June. *The Boundaries of the Soul.* Garden City, NJ: Anchor/Doubleday 1973.

Spiegel, Shalom. *The Last Trial: on the Legends and Lore of the Command to Abraham to Offer Isaac as a Sacrifice.* New York: Schocken 1969.

Spiegelman, J. Marvin and Jacobson, Abraham, Editors. *A Modern Jew in Search of a Soul*. Phoenix, AR: Falcon Press 1986.

Sproul, Barbara. *Primal Myths: Creating the World*. San Francisco: Harper & Row 1979.

Steinsaltz, Adin. *The Strife of the Spirit*. Northvale, NJ: Jason Aronson, Inc. 1988.

Steinsaltz, Adin. *The Essential Talmud*. New York: Basic Books 1976.

Stone, Merlin. *When God Was A Woman*. San Diego, CA: Harvest/HBJ 1976.

Strassfeld, M., and Strassfeld, S.. *The Third Jewish Catalog*. Philadelphia: Jewish Publication Society 1980.

Strassfeld, M., and Strassfeld, S. *The Second Jewish Catalog*. Philadelphia: Jewish Publication Society 1976.

Suars, Carlo. *Sepher Yetsira, The*. Boulder, CO: Shambhala 1976.

Talmage, Frank E., Editor. *Disputation and Dialogue: Readings in the Jewish-Christian Encounter*. New York: Ktav 1975.

Talmud, The. Epstien, I, transl. London: Soncino 1953.

Talmud Bavli (Heb.) (Babylonian Talmud, 20 vols to date). Steinsaltz, Adin, editor. Jerusalem: Israeli Talmudic Publishing Institute 1974.

Talmud Bavli (Heb.) (Babylonian Talmud, 20 vols). Vilna Edition. Jerusalem: Misrad HaDatot 1968.

Tanakh: A New Translation of the Holy Scriptures According the the Traditional Hebrew Text. Philadelphia: Jewish Publications Society 1985.

Tart, Charles, Editor. *Altered States of Consciousness*. Garden City, NY: Anchor/Doubleday 1972.

Tart, Charles. *Open Mind, Discriminating Mind*. San Francisco: Harper & Row 1989.

Tart, Charles, Editor. *Transpersonal Psychologies*. New York: Harper Colophon 1977.

Tart, Charles. *Waking Up: Overcoming the Obstacles to Human Potential*. Boston: Shambhala 1987.

The Metsudah Siddur (Heb/Eng, "The Mesudah Prayerbook, 2 vols)". New York: Metsudah 1981.

Tillich, Paul. *The Courage to Be*. New Haven: Yale 1952.

Tishby, I. *Mishnat HaZohar* (Heb. 2 Vols.). Jerusalem: Musad Bialik 1961.

Trachtenberg, Joshua. *Jewish Magic and Superstition*. Philadelphia: Jewish Publication Society 1961.

Trachtenberg, Joshua. *The Devil and the Jews: The Medieval Conception of the Jew and its Relation to Modern Antisemitism*. New York: Harper Torchbook 1943.

Underhill, Evelyn. *Mysticism*. New York: Dutton 1961.

Underhill, Evelyn. *Practical Mysticism*. New York: Dutton 1943.

Upanishads, The. Transl by Juan Mascaro. Baltimore: Penguin Books 1965.

Van Der Leeuw, G. *Religion in Essence and Manifestation* (2 vols). New York: Harper Torch 1963.

Vatsyayana. *The Kama Sutra of Vatsyayana*. New York: G.P. Putnam's Sons. 1963.

Waite, A. E. *The Holy Kabbalah*. Secaucus, NJ: University Books, Inc. 1969.

Watts, Alan. *Nature, Man and Woman*. New York: Random House 1958.

Watts, Alan. *Psychotherapy East and West*. New York: New American Library 1963.

Weiner, Herbert. *9 = Mystics*. New York: Hold, Rinehart and Winston 1969.

Weisel, Elie. *A Jew Today*. New York: Random 1978.

Weisel, Elie. *Four Hasidic Masters and their Struggle against Melancholy*. Notre Dame: Univ of Notre Dame Press 1978.

Weisel, Elie. *One Generation After*. New York: Random House 1979.

Weisel, Elie. *Somewhere a Master: Further Hasidic Portraits and Legends*. New York: Summit Books 1981.

Weisel, Elie. *Souls on Fire*. New York: Vintage/Random House 1972.

Weiss-Rosmarin, Trude. *Judaism and Christianity: The Differences*. New York: Jonathan David 1943.

Werblowsky, R.J.Zwi. *Joseph Karo: Lawyer and Mystic*. Philadelphia: Jewish Publication Society 1977.

Wilber, Ken, Editor. *Holographic Paradigm and Other Paradoxes, The*. Boulder, CO: Shambhala 1982.

Wilhelm, Hellmut. *Change: Eight Lectures on the I Ching*. Princeton, NJ: Bollingen/Princeton University Press 1960.

Williams, Strephon Kaplan. *Jungian Senoi Dreamwork Manual*. Berkeley, CA: Journey Press 1980.

Williams, Strephon Kaplan. *The Practice of Personal Transformation: a Jungian Approach*. Berkeley, CA: Journey Press 1985.

Winkler, Gershon. *Dybbuk*. New York: The Judaica Press 1981.

Winkler, Gershon. *Golem of Prague*. New York: The Judaica Press 1980.

Woocher, Jonathan. *Sacred Survival: The Civil Religion of American Jews* Bloomington, IN: Indiana University Press 1986.

Yoganada, Paramahansa. *The Autobiography of a Yogi*. Los Angeles: Self-Realization Fellowship 1946, 1974.

Zeligs, Dorothy. *Psychoanalysis and the Bible*. New York: Block Pub Co. 1974.

Zimmer, Heinrich. *Philosophies of India*. Cleveland, OH: World Publishing Co. 1951.

Zohar, The: Parashat Pinhas, P. Berg, transl. Jerusalem: Research Center for Kabbalah 1986.

Zohar, The. Sperling, H, and Simon, M, transl. London: Soncino 1934.

Zohar: the Book of Enlightenment. D. Matt, Transl. New York: Paulist Press 1983.

Index

SIGO PRESS

SIGO PRESS publishes books in psychology
which continue the work of C.G. Jung, the great
Swiss psychoanalyst and founder of analytical
psychology. Each season SIGO brings out a small
but distinctive list of titles intended to make a
lasting contribution to psychology and human
thought. These books are invaluable reading for
Jungians, psychologists, students and scholars
and provide enrichment and insight to general
readers as well. In the Jungian Classics Series,
well-known Jungian works are brought back into
print in popular editions.

Other Titles from Sigo Press

Recovering from Incest *by Evangeline Kane*

Longing for Paradise *by Mario A. Jacoby*

Emotional Child Abuse *by Joel Covitz*

Dreams of a Woman *by Shelia Moon*

Androgyny *by June Singer*

The Dream-The Vision of the Night *by Max Zeller*

Sandplay Studies *by Bradway et al.*

Symbols Come Alive in the Sand *by Evelyn Dundas*

Inner World of Childhood *by Frances G. Wickes*

Inner World of Man *by Frances G. Wickes*

Inner World of Choice *by Frances G. Wickes*

Available from your local bookseller. If unavailable, you may contact SIGO PRESS, 25 New Chardon Street, #8748A, Boston, Massachusetts, 02114. tel. (508) 281-4722. FAX (508) 283-6060.

In Australia, Gemcraft Books, Upstairs 291-293, Watteltree Road, East Malvern, Vic., Tel. (03) 509-1666, FAX (03) 500-9475